HAUNTED YARMOUTH

HAUNTED YARMOUTH

GHOSTS AND LEGENDS FROM THE CAPE

PAUL COTE
WITH DUNCAN OLIVER
AND THE HISTORICAL SOCIETY OF OLD YARMOUTH

Published by Haunted America
A Division of The History Press
Charleston, SC 29403
www.historypress.net

First published 2008

Manufactured in the United Kingdom

ISBN 978.1.59629.430.1

Library of Congress Cataloging-in-Publication Data

Cote, Paul.
Haunted Yarmouth : ghosts and legends from the Cape / Duncan Oliver, Paul
Cote, and the Historical Society of Old Yarmouth.
p. cm.
ISBN 978-1-59629-430-1
1. Ghosts--Massachusetts--Yarmouth. 2. Haunted places--Massachusetts-
-Yarmouth. I. Cote, Paul B. (Paul Benjamin) II. Historical Society of Old
Yarmouth. III. Title.
BF1472.U6O59 2008
133.109744'92--dc22
2008009933

This book is dedicated to the memory of Jack Braginton-Smith. Curmudgeon and Cape Cod legend, he was a published writer, outstanding historian and collector of historic memorabilia. The Historical Society of Old Yarmouth greatly appreciates the contributions Jack made to the organization. May his memory forever live on.

The preponderance of ghost stories and other mystical tidbits found in local folklore is intimately tied to the area's rich history. The drama of lives spent at sea and the struggles of early colonists to survive in a new land contributed to a vivid human panorama that sometimes suggested otherworldly influences.

An 1839 etching of Yarmouth in John Barber's book, *Historical Collections*. The view is looking west and the church is located on what is now known as the Yarmouth Common.

CONTENTS

ACKNOWLEDGEMENTS

The following individuals did the majority of work on the first edition published in 2006. It is their efforts that have made this second book possible.

Historical society researchers and writers: Nancy Cacioppo, Joel Chaison, Donna Cote, Sally Jackson, Duncan Oliver, Wendy Prange and Maureen Rukstalis.

Additional writers: Debbie Gray, M.J. Mulhern, Ruth Weissberger, Robert Wilkens, Rick Jones, Chris Moriarty, Katherine Beasley, Lynne Duquette, Claudette Bookbinder, Pat Tafra and Mary Bray.

Thanks to each of you for your time and effort, and congratulations on a job well done. If during the editing process I altered the story's intent or your writing style, please forgive me. There are three people that deserve special thanks: Duncan Oliver for his guidance and help in editing this book, and Carol Oliver and Donna Cote for their proofreading and suggestions.

—Paul Cote, Editor

We would like to thank the many people who were interviewed during the preparation of this book. Their help enabled us to establish the existence of the stories and provided encouragement for our researchers to dig deeper into the stories' backgrounds.

Included in this list are: the staff at HSOY, Claire Gonet, Helen Pond, John Silver, Ann Johnson, Theresa Barbo, Jaclyn Johnson, Priscilla Gregory, Mac Perna, Johanna Crosby, Ruth Weissberger, Beth Flanagan, Yarmouth Police Department, Dick and Allie Weckler, Elizabeth Perera, Dan Lovely, Caroline Ellis, Marcia Mellor, Bud Groskopf, Judy and Bill Barnatt, Sally White, John Sears, Barbara Adams, Debbie Gray, M.J. Mulhern, Pat Tafra, Jack Braginton-Smith, Haynes Mahoney, Bo Dandison, Barbara Breidenbach, Rick Jones, Chris Moriarty, Ben Muse, Paul Noonan, Claudette Bookbinder, Susan Moeller, Laurel Galvin, Suzanne

Courcier, Bob Wilkins, Betsy Embler Snow, Elizabeth Embler, Dick Morgan, Doris Cipolla, Simpkins School administration, Windsor Nursing Home administration, Pat Anderson, Dot Henion, Laurence Barber, Walter Chapin, Bill and Stephanie Wright, Roger Cash, Jessica McConnell, Katherine Beasley, Bob Davis, Rosalie Swansey, Florence Galaska, Les Campbell, Jerry Donnellan, Virginia Haskell, Charles Baxter, Carol Oliver, Eleanor Talbot, Lucy Perera-Adams, Lynne Duquette and Paul Cook. A special thanks goes to Ted Weissberger for his technical assistance.

—Historical Society of Old Yarmouth

This is a project of the Historical Society of Old Yarmouth.

INTRODUCTION

It all started with a line in Ella Bray's book *All Around the Common*, first published in 1937. On page twelve, she wrote that all but one of the houses around the Yarmouth Port Common were reputed to have ghosts. Over the years, many stories have been recited and some have been written down, but few have been published. We thought a compilation of the stories would make for an interesting read, and so began this project.

Our researchers began looking for and recording local folklore and tales of the supernatural. We were interested in not only the stories, but also in what people in Yarmouth thought about ghosts. As we became more engaged, we expanded the search to cover additional towns on the Cape. Interestingly, we found three groups of people: those who have experienced an unexplained occurrence; those who believe in the supernatural but may not have experienced an event; and those who have created a "logical" explanation for what they have witnessed. We were also interested in why people believe there are ghosts or beings with magical powers.

The historical society published its first book on ghosts, myths and legends in 2006. After that publication, additional stories were made available to our researchers. People added to previous stories and new research uncovered others. Thus, we began this second book. We incorporated new stories, updated existing stories with additional information and kept some of the better stories from the original book.

Some homeowners were hesitant to list their home addresses. They asked that we not identify the house as a condition for printing their stories. We have complied with each and every request and respect their privacy. We appreciate their allowing us to use their experiences.

The historical society researchers were quite skeptical about the stories at first. But, in the words of one of them, "You either believe in ghosts or you don't." It is really not that simple. Wendy Prange, a historical society researcher/ writer, wrote the following:

> *As a non-believer I gathered and read these stories with casual indifference. However, because of the honesty and sincerity of the experiences, I began to realize many of the stories were not coincidental, far fetched or dream related tales. They have such intense zeal and sense of*

reality, that I was convinced what had taken place, really happened. It is fascinating to read about the supernatural against the setting of old Cape Cod already so entrenched in history, surrounded by tales of the sea, ghosts, folk and witch lore. Whether you believe in ghosts or not this is a wonderful read that takes you through a myriad of situations and will definitely be entertaining.

While the authenticity of the stories can not be verified (we'll leave the question of believability to you, the reader) the Historical Society of Old Yarmouth has researched the historical data and believes it is accurate based on the information available at the time of publishing.

The Historical Society of Old Yarmouth (HSOY) continues to collect yarns, anecdotes and tales about Cape Cod. If you have a story, please share it. Write your story down and send it to HSOY at PO Box 11, Yarmouth Port, MA 02675.

ON THE COVER

FRONT COVER
The Swedenborgian Church

From the 1830s up to the end of the Victorian era, there was a spiritualist movement in this country in which followers attempted to communicate with those who had departed this life. Losses experienced during the Civil War had left many individuals bereft and seeking solace. The country's first lady, Mary Todd Lincoln, attempted to communicate with her beloved son Willie, who had died in the White House at the age of twelve. On at least one occasion, Abraham Lincoln attended one of the séances.

Many famous members of the transcendental movement, including Henry James, Bronson Alcott and Ralph Waldo Emerson, shared many of the philosophical tenets of the Swedenborgian. There was a strong belief in an afterlife, in which it was believed that one would reunite with loved ones for all time. It was logical, therefore, to attempt to gain "contact" with the deceased, since they were just living "away."

In 1830, young Caleb Reed, just out of Harvard, brought these teachings to Yarmouth. Many Yarmouth residents followed the custom of the day by attending séances in private homes within the village. As membership grew, they moved from private homes to the second floor of the Knowles store. When the new store was built (now the Parnassus Book Shop), they met there. Some say the second floor of the store was specifically built for the Swedenborgian worshipers.

The church was built in 1870 by the Swedenborgian congregation, a group of residents who followed the teaching of a seventeenth-century theologian named Emmanuel Swedenborg. Some have viewed him as the father of the spiritualist movement. The Swedenborgian church helped to fill the spiritual needs of Yarmouth's people.

Because of these beliefs, and the fact that some members believed they had contacted the departed while at church, we have included the story. Although we do not have any firsthand accounts of ghosts in this location, Ella Bray mentioned it had ghosts. Could they be departed Swedenborgian members and their families? Or was it Ira Ryder checking on "his Building." Read more on Ira Ryder in the chapter "All Around the Common—Yarmouth Port."

The Yarmouth Port Common looking toward the Swedenborgian church. This is the common Ella Bray referred to as having ghosts in every house but one.

BACK COVER

Ellen Bray

Ella's book, *All Around the Common*, was the inspiration for this book. Her stories about ghosts piqued our interest and started the researchers on their journey.

ALL AROUND THE COMMON—
YARMOUTH PORT

Today's Yarmouth Port was originally two separate villages with the boundary line just east of the common: Yarmouth Port to the west and Yarmouth to the east. It was at this point in history that the town's people referred to the main road (now Old King's Highway) as "Down Street" and "Up Street," with Down Street being Yarmouth Port and Up Street being Yarmouth. Both villages had their own commons and their own churches on or near the commons. The following stories take place around the Yarmouth Port Common.

1 STRAWBERRY LANE
Captain Matthews House

During the nineteenth century, this home was known as the Matthews house. Captain George Matthews and his extended family lived there during the nineteenth and early twentieth centuries. George was known to be somewhat cantankerous—he even objected when the neighborhood wanted to fill in the pond. He said he liked the pond, he

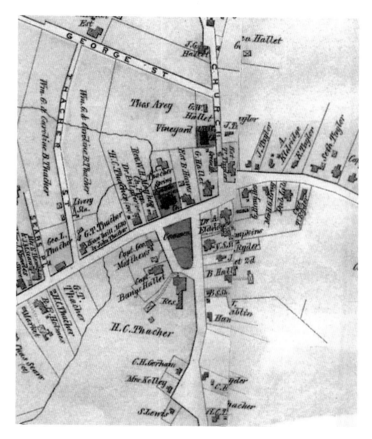

An 1880 map of Yarmouth Port Common. All of the houses in this area that are reputed to have ghosts are seen on this map.

hadn't noticed its smell and, furthermore, the pond held fond childhood memories for him. Somewhat later, the pond was filled in, creating what is now the Common.

Although no one has ever noticed the ghost of old George, either in the house or around the Common, Ella Bray, in her book *All Around the Common*, wrote about a ghost. Ella was Captain Matthews's granddaughter and she had summered in the house while growing up. Later in her life, this became her permanent residence.

When later owners moved into the house, they found an empty portmanteau or suitcase and an old wedding dress in the attic. These were the only items in the house. When they sold the house, out of respect for the former residents, they left the two items as they had found them in the attic.

But the attic just may be the key to Ella's mysterious ghost. Captain George Matthews's wife, Alice Hallet, never liked the hip roof on the house and she pestered her husband to change it. He refused. One time, while he was at sea on his vessel the *National Eagle*, his wife took matters into her own hands. She hired carpenters to change the roofline. When he returned, she may have exclaimed, "Honey, I raised the roof!" There is no record of what George said to her, but the roof remained.

Could Ella have seen, or heard, the ghost of her grandfather? Was he looking for the pond? Maybe he was trying to figure out how to get his old roof back.

8 STRAWBERRY LANE
The Edward Gorey House

This house was originally built in 1820 by Captain Edmund Hawes. After he was lost at sea, the house was purchased by Nathaniel Simpkins and his wife, the daughter of Henry C. Thacher. The Thachers owned the major house on the Common at 17 Strawberry Lane. After the Civil War, this area became the social center of Yarmouth Port. The Thachers built a golf course behind their house and had a large, two-story clubhouse that was used for social functions.

Number 8 Strawberry Lane remained in the Simpkins/Thacher families and was used as a summer home well into the twentieth century. Edward Gorey discovered the house in 1979. He purchased it and spent several years fixing it up before he moved in. Gorey was a "friend" to all animals. Even after moving in, the house continued to have raccoons living on the third floor. They would enter and exit by a broken window. Gorey fixed the window only after the raccoons had vacated the house.

Gorey's closest relative, a cousin, was asked if Edward Gorey believed in ghosts. She said that "Ted" had never mentioned any occurrences to her, and she didn't think he believed in them. She recalled an incident that happened before Gorey moved into 8 Strawberry Lane. He was living in Barnstable, at his cousin's family home. A friend was visiting and mentioned something about seeing an apparition. No further comments were made about the incident.

There are two occurrences that suggest that Gorey was aware of mysterious happenings within his home. In 1994, he mentioned to a visitor the strange disappearance of all the finials from his lamps, along with his collection of tiny teddy bears.

The second instance involved his cats. Gorey had a collection of cats that shared his life and had free run of the furniture. The number varied up to six, but if a stray showed up at his door, it was immediately welcomed. Gorey remembered a time when all the cats were on a couch and suddenly "everyone turned," eyes opening wide, as if someone, or something, unseen had entered the room. After a few seconds, the cats returned to normal.

There have been instances in which ghosts were both felt and heard, but not seen. After he died, Gorey's house became the Edward Gorey Museum. Barbara Breidenbach, who helps run the gift shop, was told a story by two guests who attended a reception at the museum. The two women were alone in the room at the back of the house when the air suddenly turned cold. Both felt a chill that raised the hair on the backs of their necks. Then they heard the floorboards creak.

"Did you feel that?" one asked the other.

"Yes, and I heard it too."

Realizing that no one else was with them, they rapidly left the room. They thought it was Edward Gorey, just checking on the people in his house. They did, however, relate the incident to Barbara.

A Little About Edward Gorey

Gorey was a noted author and illustrator. He designed both the set and the costumes for the Broadway play *Dracula*. He received a Tony Award for his costume designs. Edward Gorey is most famous for his introduction to the PBS *Mystery Theatre*.

Although Gorey may not have believed in ghosts or other supernatural occurrences, his writings were often tied to the occult. He even had his favorite ghost stories printed—stories such as "The Disrespectful Summons," which was about the devil; "The Eclectic Abecedarium," which speaks for itself; and "The Tuning Fork," which is about sea monsters. As an artist, he often drew ghosts and other spirits. The cover for the book *Witches and Warlocks—Tales of Black Magic Old and New* is filled with sea monsters, mermaids and mermen. Unfortunately, it is now out of print, although many other books by Gorey are available at the Edward Gorey Museum. Edward Gorey died in 2000. His house, now the museum, is dedicated to the preservation and memories of Mr. Edward Gorey.

11 STRAWBERRY LANE

The Captain Bangs Hallet House
Ghost or Prankster?

The Captain Bangs Hallet house originally had a store attached to the front half of the house. The section of the

The Edward Gorey House. Formerly a ship captain's home and later a summer home; it is only natural that spirits lurk here.

building containing the store was later relocated and the front of the house was rebuilt. Two sea captains have subsequently owned the house. Captain Knowles, the first captain to own the house, swapped houses with Captain Bangs Hallet in 1863. Bangs Hallet, for whom the house is named, owned it for the longest period of time.

Over the years, the house has been the setting for three unexplained occurrences. The first involves lights that turn off and thermostats that are turned down in winter. Some

Number 11 Strawberry Lane, Yarmouth Port. Known as Captain Bangs Hallet house, the photo shows the captain on the front porch.

attribute this to the frugal ways of Anna Hallet, Captain Bangs Hallet's wife. She was very thrifty, and perhaps she has not come to terms with lights left on in unused rooms or warm temperatures in winter.

Sometimes doors seem to close and creaking or "footsteps" can be heard. Some attribute this to drafts in the front section of the house, while others believe Thomas Thacher, the storeowner, is looking for the store that was moved after his death.

Another unexplained phenomenon is centered on things that are moved. Nothing is ever missing—things are just moved to a different location. When put back to their "original" locations, they may again be rearranged. There are no thoughts as to who might be doing this. Some feel it is a ghost; others, the doubters, feel it may be a person or persons who use the house and like seeing things arranged in different ways. When asked, no one admits to having knowledge of the changes.

A Little History on Captain Bangs Hallet's House

The Captain Bangs Hallet house (owned by the Historical Society of Old Yarmouth) has undergone significant changes over the years. The house was originally Thomas Thacher's store in the early 1800s. A smaller, older building was attached to it in the rear. After Thomas died in the 1830s, the store portion of the building was cut off and moved to where the Parnassus Book Shop is presently located on Route 6A. When the Parnassus building was constructed in the 1850s, the store was moved again, this time to 39 Summer Street, where it resides today.

The cellar hole remained open for several years before the front of the house was rebuilt in the 1840s. When Bangs Hallet died in 1893, the Thacher family purchased the property and used it as an annex for summer guests until the

1950s. In 1956, Guido Perera, the grandson of Henry C. Thacher, and his family gave to the Historical Society of Old Yarmouth the house and fifty-one acres of land that formerly held Henry C. Thacher's nine-hole golf links. Today, the house is maintained as a museum. Included on the grounds are the Kelley Chapel, the gatehouse, the blacksmith shop, the Gorham Cobbler Shop (administration offices of the Historical Society of Old Yarmouth) and walking trails.

A sketch of Yarmouth Port Common with the Captain Bangs Hallet house in the background. The fence was put there in spite of a 1686 requirement that the common never be fenced. Are there ghosts of the original proprietors around the common that are still angry about the fence?

17 STRAWBERRY LANE

Henry C. Thacher House
Cold and Angry

Contractor Dan Lovely was hired by the Perera family in the fall of 2002 to do some heavy demolition and rebuilding on the second floor of their home at 17 Strawberry Lane. Lawrence Perera is the great-grandson of Henry C. Thacher. After work was completed each day, Lovely would clean up the area where they were working and then check the rest of the house before leaving.

Each time he entered the upstairs front bedroom, he felt odd sensations, like someone was there. There was a feeling of tension in the room—something you feel when someone is angry. The room felt really cold—there was a noticeable drop in temperature even though no windows were open.

Dan felt the need to say something and so he told the room, "Things will look better than ever when we're done." A couple of other times he felt similar sensations in the room while cleaning up, but never quite as strongly. It seemed to him that there was less anger and tension. No one else was ever there to witness these sensations.

Dan mentioned his experiences to the owner of the house, Elizabeth Perera. She said it was not the first time someone had that feeling in the room.

Dan knew there was a door to the attic off that room. Only once did he start to go up there, and he got the distinct feeling that something didn't want him around. There was never anything to see or hear—only a feeling—but Dan didn't want to tempt fate.

When the room was finished, Dan walked back into the room, not only feeling pride at the work accomplished, but also hoping that maybe, just maybe, the ghost might speak to him, maybe even say, "Job well done," or something like that.

It didn't happen, but Dan did notice that the room had a different feel. There was no longer the feeling of anger or tension, and the room was as warm as the rest of the house. Dan realized that the ghost had spoken to him in the only way it could, and he left satisfied.

Who could the ghost have been? The family isn't sure, but there is a clue at the house next door, the Bangs Hallet house. There are three boards with writing on them on display. One came from 17 Strawberry Lane, another from Hallet's store on Old King's Highway and a third from the Swedenborgian church. Some years ago, the Pereras did some renovation work on their house. During construction, the molding had been removed, and on the back of one piece of molding was written: "no Drafting in Mass quota full—Ira Ryder Sept 18 1864—Beautiful Day—Working All Alone." Perhaps Ira Ryder was checking the Pereras' house to make sure the repairs and rebuilding were up to his standards.

A Little About Ira Ryder, A Carpenter

After this story was first written, a person living farther "down street" on Old King's Highway mentioned that someone had signed the bottom of one of the drawers in his house. Whose signature was it? Ira Ryder's of course. But who was this Ira Ryder?

Ira Ryder was born in Yarmouth on December 28, 1832. He was the son of Reuben and Harriot (Taylor) Ryder Jr. He married his wife, Emily (we don't know her maiden name), and they had two children, Gracie and Clara H. It would appear that Ira married later in life than most men, for both children were born after the Civil War; Gracie was born when Ira was thirty-four, and Clara when he was thirty-seven.

Ira spent his whole life in Yarmouth, working as a carpenter. He was mentioned earlier for having written on a piece of molding that he installed in 1864 at 17 Strawberry Lane. His signature also appears on a drawer bottom in a house near Pine Street. Both of these houses have experienced ghosts, both have gone through major renovation projects and both experienced the strongest occurrences during the renovations.

Ryder also wrote on at least two additional boards. One of these boards was given to the Historical Society in 1975 by Matthews C. Hallet. The inscription was written in 1868 and it states:

30

CONNECTICUT LOAF CAKE.

Three cupfuls of warm milk, one of sugar, one of yeast; mix to a stiff batter and let it rise over night; then add three cupfuls of sugar, two of shortening, part butter and part lard, and the whites of two eggs well beaten. Work the whole together and beat briskly until thoroughly light; add three cupfuls of raisins and citron, mace or nutmeg, cinnamon, grated orange peel, and lemon for flavoring. Put it in the pans; let it rise about one hour and bake in a moderate oven one hour and a quarter. This quantity makes three loaves. — MRS. J. W. DODGE.

CHOCOLATE CAKE.

One and a half cupfuls of sugar, one and a half of butter, three eggs; beat the yolks and whites separately, one half a cup of milk, one teaspoonful of soda, two teaspoonfuls of cream of tartar; add to this one cup of chocolate, which has been melted over the teakettle, three tablespoonfuls of scalded milk, three of sugar, and one and a half of flour. Frost with white frosting. — MISS LOUISE G. HALLET.

CHOCOLATE CAKE. —FIRST PART.

One cup of sugar, one large tablespoonful of butter, one teaspoonful of vanilla, one half cup of milk, one and three quarters cups of flour; mix all together.

SECOND PART.

Melt two squares of chocolate, one half cup of milk, yolk of one egg; boil till it thickens, add one teaspoonful of soda dissolved in a little water; mix with first part and bake. — MRS. IRA RYDER.

NUT CAKE.

Two and a half cupfuls of sugar, one of butter, one of milk, four of flour, five eggs, the yolks and whites

Ira Ryder's wife donated this recipe to a local cookbook. Ira liked chocolate cake almost as much as quality carpentry.

Ira Ryder—Yarmouth Dec 15th 1868—Snow on the ground but warm. George Kalley & Dustin Eldridge putting up vane—I am now 35 years and 11 month 17 days old—Pop goes the weasel

Interestingly, the board came from some other location and was used in the construction of the store; something not unusual at the time, for lumber was often reused. Hallet's store was built with much fanfare in the 1880s—the inscription on the board was dated 1868. The names of the people who actually built the store are known, and Ira Ryder was not one of the workmen. What isn't known is the location of the building where the board originated. The inscription mentions installing a "vane" (weather vane), which may indicate it could have been a barn.

The last board came from the Swedenborgian church. It was found during the renovation of the church in 2007.

256 OLD KING'S HIGHWAY

The Red House
Strange Goings-on (By a Former Owner)

Strange goings-on started the evening we moved into the old Thacher Gorham house at 256 Old King's Highway. The dining room light insisted on flickering, especially during dinner. It continued until the old wallpaper was stripped and the room painted. Could the spirit have had a dislike for the wallpaper?

There is a small pantry off the kitchen, overlooking wetlands that always had a feeling of sadness. This was the only place where you could find the remains of a real lock—probably any and all valuables were stored therein. The shelves were perfect for dishes and glassware. At one point, a two-inch lip was added to the front of the shelves to protect glasses from slipping off. During a coffee break, while we were sitting quietly in the kitchen, a wineglass decided to hop over the lip and fall about four feet to the floor, unbroken.

I must admit that the upstairs den, which we converted to an art studio, had a very friendly feeling. It had previously been used as a music room and study by the former owner, a minister. This has nothing to do with ghost stories, but once I started to build a garden in the back, a beautiful wisteria bush appeared out front and quickly crept up the front of the house. I questioned longtime neighbors and friends of earlier owners and no one remembers ever seeing wisteria on the property.

Editor's note: The former owner sent these reminiscences by email since she and her husband now live in New York. The email was received scrambled, complete with little boxes and tildes, and with sentences in the wrong order. It took nearly an hour to decipher it. I sent her a thank-you and told her what had happened. She sent another email with the same material, this time using a different format. Interestingly, this was also scrambled, but not in the same manner as the first. The sentences were in a different order as well.

The Historical Society of Old Yarmouth used this story in a program it presented in July 2006. The material had been totally retyped, and then emailed to another member. Again, it came though scrambled, just as the previous emails. Could the ghosts at 256 Old King's Highway have the capability to disrupt today's electronic communications?

A Boy Named Albert

During the 1920s and lasting into the 1950s, the Thorpe family lived in what was known as the Red House at 256 Hallet Street (Old King's Highway), next door to the parsonage of the Swedenborgian church. Thorpe worked for the Thacher family as the gardener of their estate. As part of his compensation, the Thorpe family received housing from the Thachers, living in the Red House.

Mr. and Mrs. Thorpe had a son named Albert, who at the age of thirteen was quite adventurous. One day in 1932 he just disappeared from home. The Thorpes became frantic and a search was executed, but Albert was not to be found. This incident became the talk of the town—had Albert Thorpe met his demise?

After several days, Mrs. Thorpe began to notice that each morning food and milk were missing from the refrigerator. Two weeks later, Albert returned home and announced

Number 256 Old King's Highway, Yarmouth Port. In this house lived Albert Thorpe, who hid in the tower of the nearby Swedenborgian church for two weeks. Some believed he may have died.

that he had been living in the tower of the Swedenborgian church. He spent his days observing life in the village, only returning home late at night for sustenance. Shocked at his behavior and certain that Albert had a mental illness, the Thorpes made an appointment for a psychiatric evaluation at Bridgewater State Hospital. Following the consultation, the psychiatrist gave the family a written report, along with a certificate saying that "Junior" was of sound mental health.

Albert returned to Yarmouth Port, proudly carrying his certificate. He would walk around the town showing off the certificate and announcing to all that "he was the only person in Yarmouth Port who had a certificate saying he was sane!"

CAPTAINS' MILE—
YARMOUTH PORT

Captains' Mile is a section of highway (Route 6A) that runs through the village of Yarmouth Port. The Historical Society of Old Yarmouth has identified fifty-five sea captains' homes in the village, forty-seven of which are located on Captains' Mile. Sea captains have played an important part in the development of Cape Cod, its history and its folklore. Many of the stories in this book relate to either sea captains or the sea. Captains' Mile is part of the National Historic District known as Old King's Highway starting in the town of Sandwich and ending in Orleans, Massachusetts.

Many of the stories in this chapter are written by the current homeowners. Some have asked that we not identify their addresses. We have honored all requests for anonymity.

176 OLD KING'S HIGHWAY

The Gorham House
A Baby

This house was built by Captain Josiah Gorham. In 1835, the *Yarmouth Register* noted, "His residence is a pretentious and substantial affair indicating that the captain was a man of means and taste."

Josiah was one of eight brothers, seven of whom went to sea. Five of them became captains. Josiah was captain of some of the finest ships that sailed from Boston. Included in this group was the *Kit Carson*, a clipper ship built at Shiverick Shipyard in East Dennis.

Gorham and his wife, Harriet Barber, had a daughter named Mary who died while still a baby. The death so upset Gorham's wife that she became mentally unbalanced.

A former owner of the home, unaware of the history, recited a story to one of Gorham's descendants about hearing a baby crying. The woman was then told the story of the tragic death of the baby and the wife's subsequent mental problems.

Is there a connection? The present owners also have a baby story.

Vision or Dream

We had just moved into the Gorham House in early June, and the building was truly a mess. There was so much repair work to be done. The renovations were so extensive that we just closed our eyes and started. Our work had begun in earnest.

It must have been a few weeks after we moved in that it happened. I was just getting into bed after a long day. My wife was sound asleep beside me, but I was still wide awake when something appeared hovering about my bed. It wasn't something, but someone.

It was a toddler, perhaps a year or two old. I couldn't tell if it was a boy or a girl because of the way it was dressed. It was wearing an outfit from years ago that made the gender indistinguishable. The outfit looked like some type of robe. Surrounding this baby was a bluish light that shone like an aura.

I felt mesmerized, or else I was just paralyzed by the sight. This vision stayed above our bed for several minutes, neither of us moving. The child just looked down at me, staring. Finally, the child left.

I kept this to myself for several weeks until, finally, I confided in my wife while we were on vacation. When I thought back on it, I began to doubt that I had been awake. It must have been a dream. But no, I was totally conscious and I did see a baby. Perhaps the child was checking out its new family. We have not seen the baby since.

361 OLD KING'S HIGHWAY

Organ Music (By the Homeowner)

Little did I know that only women could hear the music. "Jesu, Joy of Man's Desiring" was being played on an organ, softly at first and then building to a crescendo until I thought I would go mad. I was in bed trying to read.

We had purchased the Cape Cod house on 6A in 1969. It had been built around 1808. In the attic we found a brass bed and a very old trunk presumably left there by a previous occupant. We were unable to determine ownership, and to this day the trunk has never been opened. We were once told that to do so would bring bad luck. Even curiosity has not tempted us to peruse the contents. The house, like most of the Capes of that era, is most interesting and charming. We later discovered the room we now use as the kitchen and the room above were brought over the ice from Nantucket by oxen and added to the existing structure.

Within a couple of months, it started. My husband and I retired to our bedroom in the front of the house; a room that had once been the parlor. Immediately, he fell asleep and loud snoring commenced. I was reading my book. Suddenly, I became aware of organ music playing in the background. Gradually, it became loud enough to recognize the hymns being played. When I mentioned it to my husband the next day, he adamantly denied hearing it and dismissed it by saying that someone probably was

Number 361 Old King's Highway, Yarmouth Port. It is in the front bedroom of this house where pipe organ music is heard. The exterior has changed little in the last one hundred years.

playing an organ across the street. No, that was not the case—the music came from inside the bedroom. I knew it was real and not in my imagination. Someone had been playing the organ in our bedroom.

From that day on, I was to hear it over and over again. And it continues, but only in the bedroom, only at night and only I hear it. Sometimes it is so loud that I have to get up and sit in the kitchen to read my book, waiting for the music to cease. There will be a break of two or three nights, and then, without warning, the music will recommence and continue for several nights in a row. Sometimes the music will be faint, but mostly it plays very loudly. It is always organ music and always hymns. The predominant piece is "Jesu, Joy of Man's Desiring."

When my son was in the second grade, I had an occasion to take him out of school early. I met with the school secretary and we chitchatted about this and that. She asked where we lived in Yarmouth. I described the location and she turned to me and said, "Doesn't the music drive you nuts?" I was speechless.

It was extremely loud the day our first grandchild was born. We had been visiting, and we came home and went to bed. As usual, I picked up my book and was about to read when the music started. It became so loud that I couldn't stand it. Finally, to my surprise, I said out loud, "Thank you very much, I enjoyed that." To my amazement the music stopped!

I have come to the conclusion that at one time someone lived in the house that played the organ. Unfortunately, anyone who would have been around at that time has passed on. Although I have made exhaustive inquiries, I have never been able to shed light upon this strange happening that continues to this day.

OLD KING'S HIGHWAY

Footsteps in the Living Room
(By the Homeowner)

Finally my dreams were coming true. I was leaving my hectic life and career in New York City behind and moving to beautiful and quiet Cape Cod.

I moved into a sea captain's home built around 1850 on historic Old King's Highway. There was much work to be done to get the house with "good bones" to shine through. But I was very determined, and the work became a pleasure. The wallpaper was stripped, the wall-to-wall carpet was removed and the natural floors were beautifully refinished. There were no shades or curtains on the windows, and most of the furniture was out of the house being re-covered. Being busy all day, and being alone, it became my habit to retire rather early.

One evening I was awakened from a deep sleep by the sound of heavy footsteps pacing back and forth from my sitting room to my living room. I glanced at the alarm clock; it was 3:00 a.m. As I was alone, I was frozen with fear. Then the footsteps ceased. But it happened again! Months later, I heard the same heavy footsteps at the same time, 3:00 a.m. This time I plucked up the courage to investigate and made it down three of the stairs, but saw nothing. Returning to my bed, I hoped there would be a next time—maybe the spirit would reveal itself. I never heard the footsteps again. But something quite different did take place.

The Baby's Room

Upstairs, behind my bedroom, there is a room that I have always referred to as the "baby's room." I don't know why, as I do not have a baby (just a lovable cocker spaniel). Overnight guests always stay in the baby's room. Two of my girlfriends told me afterward how fast they had fallen asleep and how peaceful their sleep had been. They both have quite different personalities and temperaments, yet each remarked how they felt "cocooned" in that room and so safe. I though it strange that they should both use this expression.

One night I was awakened from the grasps of a deep sleep, again at 3:00 a.m. A baby was crying. For some unknown reason I knew it was a girl crying and that the cries were coming from the baby's room. I felt a real urgency to get to the baby and take care of her. Of course, once fully awake, I realized there was no baby in the baby's room.

Months later, I took a walk to the Ancient Cemetery in Yarmouth. Here I discovered the gravesite of the sea captain who had lived in my house. Alongside the grave was another smaller grave, for a baby girl who had died around the age of one. A sudden chill swept through my body.

I am pleased to tell you that the house is calm and peaceful these days and I am so happy here. I must say that I never feel quite alone, but only in the best of ways.

OLD KING'S HIGHWAY
Uncle Lester (By the Homeowner)

We live in an old sea captain's house that was built around 1840. One day about fifteen years ago, while I was cleaning, I walked through my dining room and smelled cigar smoke. It was in one particular area, in a single column from floor to ceiling. No one in the house smoked. When my daughter came home from school, she also smelled the cigar smoke. That evening, my husband came home, and he, too, could smell the smoke. It did not subside until the following day.

We were curious, so we talked to our neighbor, whose grandfather was the original owner. We asked whether, to his knowledge, anyone had smoked in the house? He came over to the house, immediately walked into the dining room and pointed to the spot where "Uncle Lester used to smoke one stinky stogie after the other." It was the exact spot where we had smelled the smoke. It has never returned, but now and then we think about Uncle Lester sitting in his Morris chair smoking his stogies. I am waiting for him to return.

Wintertime Wonders

Another incident happened during the wintertime. In one of the upstairs bedrooms, there is a small wood stove that we enjoy. It has isinglass in the front so we can see the fire. One evening we lit the stove. When I got up in the middle of the night, it had gone out and the room was cool. I left the room for a short while, and when I returned, I laid down to go back to sleep. Suddenly, this strange light appeared on one of my two window shades. It was a rectangular white light on the inside of the shade.

Just as I thought this was very interesting, the stove, which had since burned out, suddenly burst into flames on the inside and started to roar. I became concerned about a possible chimney fire, when suddenly the fire went out—turned off like a light switch. It was completely dark and then I heard it, the distinct sound of an old Model T driving away—*chug-a-chug-a-chug-a-chug-a-chug*.

Surprisingly, I was not scared and did not discuss what had transpired with my husband. A couple of days later, it crossed my mind that if I told anyone what had happened they would have put me in the loony bin. Eventually I confided in my husband. He's an engineer, so he knows all about these things and why they happen. I must say he was condescending.

He rationalized the light on the window: "Perhaps the police were coming by and for some reason they had a searchlight and they happened to pan across the front of our house. That's why you saw the light." So I asked, "What about the stove fire?" "Build up of gases and a spark," he remarked. "What about the sound of the Model T?" For once, he was at a loss for words, but he looked at me strangely.

The built-up gases might have been true. Perhaps there was a spark. Then I started to think about the light on the window shade, the light that stayed for just a few seconds. I realized that we have blackout shades, so if a searchlight were panning across the front of the house, I would have only seen slivers of light down the sides of the shade. Evidently, the light was coming from the inside the room. It had to be. The whole thing—light on the shade and fire in the stove—lasted about twenty seconds. I don't know why, but I do know that I was not afraid.

Music at Night

It was wintertime again, and my husband and I had just laid our heads on the pillows. The house was nice and quiet, when suddenly we heard many bars of a Victorian ditty playing on a familiar—yet not-in-this-lifetime familiar— musical instrument. It was not a harpsichord, a piano or an organ, but something like that. It seemed to emanate from the dining room. My husband heard it, as did our daughter.

Finally, my husband was able to accept my insistence of strange happenings in the house. There were other smaller "happenings," but never anything scary. I do vividly recall that our dog would occasionally sit at the foot of the stairs looking upwards as if waiting for someone to come down. This would only happen when we were alone in the house.

The activity stopped once our daughter moved out. I understand that the "energy" can gravitate toward a teenager who acts like a lightning rod to the psychic activity. My daughter has been gone for over twelve years, and since her departure we have neither seen nor heard anything.

Occasionally we moved or added pictures to a room. For no apparent reason they would be askew and we needed to straighten them. We were constantly straightening pictures. This did not happen in all rooms, and it only happened now and then. I believe it is the action of "people" letting us know they do not care for the cosmetic changes that were taking place in the house. But even with the recent and rather large addition to the house, nothing unusual has taken place. Finally, it seems everything is where they want it to be.

OLD KING'S HIGHWAY

I Saw a Dog (By a Participant)

It started with what we called "the coven." Even though this term is often linked with witches, *Merriam-Webster* defines it as "a collection of individuals with similar interests or activities." That made it an appropriate name for our little group of neighborhood women. We would meet monthly, either at a restaurant or a member's home, for "girl's night out." It was at one of our member's home that it happened.

We were in our hostess's lovely old sea captain's home on 6A in Yarmouth Port. One of the women offered to read tarot cards, which seemed like the perfect entertainment for the night. As we were all gathered around the dining room table taking turns having our fortunes read, the woman who was reading the cards suddenly looked up and said, "I just saw a dog." She pointed to the bottom of the staircase and said, "There was a dog sitting right there." However, the owner of the house didn't own a dog.

The home is a Greek revival with three staircases. The dog was "seen" at the bottom of the center staircase near the dining room. Naturally, everyone turned in the direction of the staircase, yet no one else saw a dog. The woman reading the tarot cards insisted that she saw a dog and it looked like a Maltese.

It was too good of a moment to let slide, so we all had a few comments to make to our tarot-card-reader-who-sees-dogs. Right in the middle of some of our best "sure you saw a dog" routines, our hostess managed to silence us all by saying, "Ladies, you're not going to believe this."

She told us that when her father was alive, he would often come to visit her, and when he did he would bring his small dog with him (the two had passed on years before). As it often is with small dogs, his dog could not climb stairs. The hostess and her husband had owned a cat. Their cat knew the dog was unable to climb the stairs, so the cat would sit on the landing halfway up the staircase looking down at the dog and teasing him. This put the dog at the bottom of the stairs, looking up, just as our tarot card reader described

The story left us all a bit stunned, as our tarot card reader did not have knowledge of our hostess's father and his dog. Yet, she saw a dog sitting in the exact location the tormented Maltese used to sit.

Could it be that her father and his beloved dog still come to visit?

371 OLD KING'S HIGHWAY
The Captain's Wife (By the Homeowner)

Have you ever had the feeling that someone was watching you? Not just the glance-around type of reaction, but an overpowering, intense feeling that makes you react quickly to see who it is. I have.

My husband and I purchased an old sea captain's home on 6A in Yarmouth Port. Since neither one of us had ever owned an older home, we became fascinated with finding out all we could about the original owner. I spent hours researching Cape Cod sea captains and their ships, looked up genealogy records, found deeds, copied all the information I had acquired and finally created a scrapbook about "My Captain." When you spend that much time on a single person you become attached to, even possessive of, him. This is why I refer to Captain Nathaniel Taylor as My Captain.

Captain Taylor commanded the schooner *Yarmouth*, a packet ship that sailed between Yarmouth and Boston. When the *Yarmouth* was sold, Captain Taylor took command of the packet *Lucy Elizabeth*. It was aboard the *Lucy Elizabeth* that a gunning accident permanently injured his arm, thus changing his life forever. Captain Taylor lost command of the ship, along with his livelihood. He opened a dry goods store behind the house, but due to the onset of the Civil War and the depressed economy, he struggled to make a living. He died bankrupt at the age of forty-nine.

After her husband's death in 1867, the courts ordered his wife, Mercy, to auction off the inventory of their store and awarded the proceeds to their creditors. When the amount didn't cover all the debts, she was ordered to auction her home. A prosperous and generous neighbor purchased her home for fifty dollars and resold it to Mercy the very same day. He held the mortgage, which enabled Mercy to continue living in the house and to raise her two children there. For the next forty-one years, until her death in 1908 at the age of eighty-seven, Mercy existed on a widow's allowance. It was while I was researching Mercy's story that the "feeling" happened.

I was standing in our kitchen, which is in what we refer to as the "new" part of the house, when it happened. As is the case with old homes, they often need renovation, and ours was no exception. When we purchased the house, there was an ell on the back, built in the 1920s, that had to be demolished. In its place, we designed a connecting room and relocated the kitchen. We built a fireplace in the kitchen using the bricks from the original well that was found under the ell when it was torn down.

Our surprise came while I was researching the house. The Historical Society of Old Yarmouth had a picture of our house taken in the 1800s. It showed the house with a connecting room leading into what appeared to be a kitchen. The location of the kitchen in the photograph, including the fireplace, was the same location as the new kitchen.

One night, while I was in the "new" kitchen standing at the sink with my back to the room, I had the most incredible feeling that someone was watching me. I literally spun around, and there she was, looking at me. She was standing in front of the icebox, only a few feet from where I stood. She started to raise her hand. Her face reflected the startled look of someone taken by surprise. From her dress, I felt this must be Mercy Taylor.

She wore a pale-colored cotton dress, possibly faded pink, with a pattern of small white flowers. It had a plain round collar and gatherers at the waist. She wore no jewelry or any other ornamentation. Her day cap came down to her ears and covered most of her dark hair. She appeared to be in her late thirties or early forties. Then she disappeared.

I can only speculate why Mercy came to visit. Could it have been the remodeling that put the kitchen back to its original location? Or was she reminiscing about her home and how it looked during happier times? I guess I will never know, as Mercy's visit was much too brief. I wish she would have stayed, as I have so many questions I would love to have asked her.

OLD KING'S HIGHWAY

Our Houseguests (By the Homeowner)

When we bought our captain's home ten years ago, we were delighted to own a piece of history. After moving into our new home, we began the usual renovations that are needed to restore hundred-year-old homes. It was then that we realized we had squatters. There was nothing mentioned in our real estate brochure, nor was there any addendum to our deed. There are, however, people who currently dwell in our home, and they intend to keep on inhabiting it.

It seems that any construction brings them out of the woodwork. I first saw "him" when we were working on the front of the house. Something woke me at about 2:00 a.m., and I saw him in my bedroom window. He wasn't outside looking in, but instead, he was sitting inside, looking east down Route 6A.

He was thirtyish, rather thin and almost gaunt, with dark hair that brushed his collar. His shirt was white with blousy arms. I could only see his torso. I sat up in bed to get a better look, but he disappeared. I thought I must have been dreaming and went back to sleep.

Footprints

As work progressed on various projects, the noises within the house seemed to become more pronounced. You could hear footsteps in the upper hall and doors slamming. But there was never anyone there, and the doors remained wide open. Often, my husband was alone in the house and he was sure that someone was walking above him.

When we began to renovate the kitchen, our houseguests were interested. The dust started flying as ceilings and walls were removed. One morning, as I climbed the stairs to the

Nineteenth-century heel prints in the dust made by unknown forces at the Captain Ezra Howes house.

bedroom, I noticed prints on the floor at the top of the stairs. I had just vacuumed the day before so I asked my husband if we had company upstairs.

He came to look, and upon examination, he determined that they were human shoe prints, heels specifically. "They aren't modern heels." He then added, "Look at the nails." I noticed that whoever had been standing there was facing the kitchen as if they could see through the wall at the worker doing the construction. I still keep checking the heels of my shoes to come up with a match for the prints. My size 6½ shoes were still too big.

Some months have passed. Someone is still walking the halls. I have heard whoever it is stomp to my bedroom door and enter the dressing room next door. My husband hears these sounds too.

It wasn't until a few weeks later that my neighbor related his tale of banging doors and lights turning on and off. We talked of similar odd events and concluded that both houses were having experiences on the same nights.

As you are driving along Route 6A, you might admire these old captains' homes. Perhaps you may envision owning one yourself—picture yourself spending summers going to the beach, walking the trails, entertaining your guests. You may even find yourself with houseguests who refuse to leave—ever.

Old King's Highway, Yarmouth. The former home of Captain Ezra Howes has seen many strange occurrences.

Blowing in the Wind

One summer, we decided to redecorate the front bedroom, an undertaking that proved to be a lengthy process. We had to sleep in a bedroom in the rear of the house. One night, I got up in the wee hours and happened to look out a window that faced our barn.

There was something billowing by the side door. At first I thought my husband had tossed one of my lace curtains over the door. I was a bit miffed, so I went to a different window to get a better view. I could see this object about a foot off the ground floating near the barn door. It was semitransparent and appeared to softly shift in the breeze, although it was a hot, steamy July night and there was no breeze.

Curiosity got the best of me. I walked down to the kitchen to get a better view. The shape radiated a soft white glow, yet I couldn't see a light source—no streetlight or neighbor's spotlight was in evidence.

The vision was almost the length of the door, which made me again think of my good lace curtain. I decided to return to bed, resolving that the next morning I would hand my husband his head on a platter for ruining a perfectly good curtain.

The next morning I awoke and immediately went to the window to verify that, indeed, the lace material was hanging on a nail. There was nothing there.

404 OLD KING'S HIGHWAY
It's All Right Sarah

Yankee spirit and ingenuity are used to describe this lovely 1700s home on 6A (Old King's Highway). This wonderful home originally stood in either Duxbury or Plymouth. In the 1800s, this house was taken apart, put on a barge and floated across the bay. A team of oxen then pulled it from the bay to its present location in Yarmouth Port. Because of this long and incredible journey, the house is said to be "flaked." The art of moving a home in this fashion is known as "flaking." Due to its unusual history, we are uncertain who the original owners were and who the ghost might have been. However, previous owners chose to name their ghostly houseguest Sarah. Sarah, an old family name, suited the friendly presence.

Sarah was what one would call a poltergeist, a spirited prankster. She liked doing playful things like closing windows and putting the toilet seat down. What she didn't like was having the guest bedroom door latched. Whenever the door to this one particular bedroom was latched, Sarah would open it during the night. The latch on the door is the old-fashioned type that you push down, exerting pressure with your thumb—not one that could easily swing open from the wind.

The owners told their guests about Sarah and suggested they leave the bedroom door unlatched. One night, a friend spent the night. She retired, latched the door and went to sleep. Not long after, the host and hostess heard the latch lift. They thought it was their guest and therefore were unconcerned until they heard her scream, "Sarah! It's all right. You can have the door open!"

At 4:45 a.m. that same night, a window slammed shut, waking everyone in the house. As in many old homes, they were the original guillotine windows, named because of the manner in which they could come crashing down.

To prevent this from happening, pieces of solid wood are placed between the sill and the bottom of the window sash. The wood was securely in place that night; nevertheless, the window slammed shut.

After breakfast, their guest tried to call her husband to tell him of her eventful night, but the phone was dead. The hostess left to use a neighbor's phone, wanting to report the problem to the telephone company. While she was at the neighbor's house, her home phone rang. It was her daughter calling—her grandmother had died at 4:45 that morning. The phone once again went dead and remained so for the rest of the day.

Unfortunately, this was not the only tragic loss the family would suffer. Their thirty-five-year-old son died in a motorcycle accident on his way to meet his wife to celebrate their first anniversary. The family flew to California, where their son lived, to attend the funeral. When they returned to their home on 6A, they noticed an empty feeling in the house. They believed the empty feeling was due to the loss of their son, even though he had never lived there. Time went on, but the feeling remained. They also noticed that Sarah's pranks had ceased and soon realized that Sarah, too, was gone. They believe that Sarah left to comfort and be with their son.

The present homeowners have neither experienced nor seen anything to remind them of Sarah.

418 OLD KING'S HIGHWAY
Phoebe's Displeasures

Captain Oliver Matthews lived in this house with his wife Phoebe from 1835 until his death in 1883. He was the captain of the brig *Isabel*. Although quite successful, he had to retire at an early age due to illness. Elixirs, medicine bottles and bottles of pills believed to be from that period were recently discovered in the chimney box.

The interior has not been seriously altered since Captain Matthews lived here. On the second floor, there is a room wallpapered with clippings from nineteenth-century magazines—the work of Phoebe while the captain was at sea in 1860. The room, known as Phoebe's Room, was recently furnished with a collection of antique dolls and toys of the period. Phoebe's Room is located on the second floor over the dining room. After the redecorating, a water leak was noticed in the dining room. It appeared to have originated from the second floor. The problem was that there was no water source or explanation as to where the water came from. The new owners remain dumbfounded.

On New Year's Day 2006, a small "Charlie Brown" Christmas tree, decorated with the owner's antique decorations and secured in a heavy, wrought-iron stand, was discovered on its side. This was a real mystery, considering the weight of the iron stand. The owners claim that the stand could not possibly have fallen over by itself.

Could it be that Phoebe was not pleased with the owner's choice of tree that year?

Apparently Phoebe and the captain like the house just the way they left it. Past owners have reported that when they attempted to repair things, their tools would disappear, although not permanently. The tools would be returned when requested. The new owners claim that they, too, are constantly missing items.

One previous owner remarked that he had observed apparitions of a sad looking man and a lady in pink. He felt they might have been the ill captain and Phoebe.

450 OLD KING'S HIGHWAY

Captain Bearse House (By the Homeowner)
The China Plate

Editor's note: Claire, the current owner, believes strongly that the unexplained occurrences she and others have experienced in the Captain Bearse House are, in fact, the good captain's way of introducing himself.

I took ownership on August 11, 2005. The house was completely emptied by the prior owner. I went to Orleans a week later and found a lovely indoor thermometer in the shape of a porthole, all brass, with the face of a sailing vessel from the eighteenth century. I placed it on the wall, and underneath I hung a souvenir china plate I had bought. The plate had a picture of a sailing captain and the name "Cape Cod."

These pieces were secured to the wall, with the plate being about five feet from the floor. There was nothing below them. I later left the house and went back to my home on the beach. When I returned the next day, the China plate was "placed" on the floor, not broken or damaged in any way.

I picked it up and hung it back on the wall—the plate's nail was still where I had put it. I would think that if a china plate fell even two feet, it would smash. This leads me to believe that it was Captain Bearse, who wanted me to know that he was in the house and recognized my tribute to him. The two pieces were hung in the 1721 hearth room, part of the original house.

Fire in the Fireplace

On three separate occasions prior to Claire moving in, people helping her noticed a small fire in the main hearth. When entering the house, they said it smelled as though someone was cooking dinner in the fireplace. The only problem was that no one had put logs in the fireplace or started a fire. Perhaps Captain Bearse was "warming" the house for them.

On another occasion, a candle that had been securely pushed into a candleholder in the evening was found laying on the floor, unbroken, the next morning. No one had been near the candle or the holder, yet the candle had moved.

Missing Glass

Another occurrence took place only recently. Claire kept her favorite garnet-colored glasses in a cabinet in the kitchen. One day, she discovered one of them was missing. A thorough search of the kitchen, including every cabinet, failed to turn up the lost glass.

Three weeks later, Claire opened a cabinet on the opposite side of the kitchen from where she stored her glasses. As she opened the door, a garnet-colored item flew by her and broke on the floor. It was the missing glass!

How did it get there? That very cabinet had been checked three weeks earlier and the glass had not been found, nor had anyone seen the glass when later using the cabinet. Claire explains the mystery by saying that it must have been the ghost of Captain John Bearse who placed the glass there. There is no other explanation.

Why him? All of the incidents seem to point to a ghost or poltergeist intent on letting the current owner know that it still resides in the house. Claire is not frightened of it—the ghost doesn't try to cause harm. The garnet glass might have simply been moved too close to the edge of the shelf.

Claire feels a presence, but she says the house feels like home. Her connection to Captain John Bearse? Both were born on the same day, May 8.

A Little History on the Captain Bearse House

Captain John Bearse owned the house from 1754 until his death in 1759. Bearse left the house to his granddaughter, Suzanna Basset. Suzanna later married Elisha Doane. It was during this time that the house became known as the Squire Doane's Tavern. Elisha Doane, an industrial person (see "57 Wharf Lane" for a related story), operated the tavern, which was known for its good times and good fare.

When Claire purchased the house, the property was still referred to as the Squire Doane's Tavern. She thought it would be better to rename the property in honor of the captain. Claire has converted the house into the Captain Bearse House and runs it as a bed-and-breakfast. Perhaps that was the reason Captain Bearse made his presence known to her.

THE REDHEADED WOMAN

There have been rumors of a ghost that lives near the Yarmouth Common (the one with the playground). There seems to be evidence of a small, redheaded woman with a hood.

Number 450 Old King's Highway, Yarmouth. The house has been commonly known as the Elisha Doane Tavern, but was renamed the Captain Bearse Inn because Bearse was the only sea captain to live in this house on Captains' Mile.

Who she was and what her relationship to Yarmouth might have been has become a subject of conjecture. Was it the young woman who drowned in a pond near here? She was from a family of redheads. Perhaps she is the redheaded ghost reportedly seen in the vicinity of the meetinghouse common. People speculated as to who this woman was, or why she gravitated to this area. Few knew the story, until now.

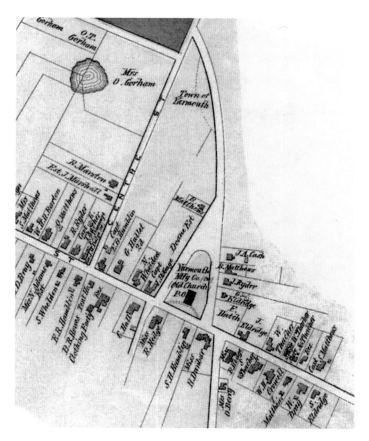

An 1880 map of Yarmouth Common. This common, farther to the east than the Yarmouth Port Common, was the location of Congregational churches from 1716 until 1870. Many ghost stories come from this area.

Several years ago, a family on Old King's Highway decided to have their elderly mother live with them. They added a wing to their home so the matriarch would have her own private quarters. While the construction was going on, the elderly woman occupied the back bedroom at the top of the staircase.

It was just about the time the construction had begun in earnest that the woman fell. She was on the staircase leading to her bedroom when she toppled to the bottom of the stairs. She was rushed to the local hospital, where she recuperated from the serious fall.

Upon hearing of the terrible accident, a next-door neighbor approached the family about the mishap. The woman was concerned about the manner in which the accident had occurred. Was there a ghost?

The family was taken aback by such a preposterous suggestion until the neighbor clarified her statement. One hundred years ago, a redheaded woman had died in this house. She fell on that stairway and broke her neck.

Some people have said that the red-haired woman divides her time between the family's home and the neighbor's house next door. You may even get a glimpse of her flitting between the two homes.

THE HOME OF AN UNDERTAKER FOR WOMEN
By Katherine Beasley, Age Thirteen

It was about mid-July, and I was spending the week at my Dad's house on 6A in Yarmouth Port. I had just finished watching *The Cosby Show* on Nick at Nite and I turned off the television and fell asleep. The next thing I knew, I heard a door slamming shut a number of times. I looked over with my barely opened eyes and the light in my closet was flashing on and off and the door was opening and closing.

I jumped out of bed and raced down the stairs to my Dad, who was sound asleep on the couch. It was about 3:00 in the morning, and I woke him up to tell him. When he went upstairs, the television was on even though I had turned it off prior to going to sleep. Everything else was silent. My Dad thought I was dreaming, but I'm sure I wasn't.

It was very strange because I live in a very old house, and the closet door has a latch. When the door was opening and closing, most of the time it didn't close so that it latched shut. Did I mention that during the 1800s our house was used by the undertaker for women?

Editor's note: Those who study ghosts and spirits say ghosts often reappear in an attempt to complete a less than satisfying event. A closet repeatedly opening and closing in a funeral home might suggest that someone wasn't satisfied with the clothing worn, or was trying to change clothes.

Whether it was Katherine's dream, as her father suggested, or an actual ghost, the situation might have been eased if someone had said, "You look fine" or "Your clothes are very appropriate." Letting a spirit know that the situation has been satisfactorily handled is one way of ending the situation.

WITHIN YARMOUTH PORT

57 WHARF LANE

Stories Told by the Homeowner
The Mirror

When we were asked if we have any ghosts in our house, I smiled and replied, "We might have a good ghost."

It has been nearly twenty years since the day Suzanne and I first saw the house. We had devoted a solid year looking, and I had about given up hope. One day, as we were about to bear left onto Thacher Shore Road, I spotted the For Sale sign. "What about that place?" I asked our realtor.

"Oh, it's too small for you."

"Too small? We only need room for me, Suzanne and the two spaniels!"

Early that afternoon, we were inside. The house had been rented for the past seven years and showed obvious signs of neglect. The walls were covered with layers of peeling wallpaper, except for those areas where chunks of plaster had fallen off and were scattered on the floor. The floors were all painted the same shade of brown, which I will describe as the color of "mud," and the trim was painted a particularly bilious shade of green.

I had been inside ten, maybe fifteen seconds tops, when I turned to Suzanne and our astonished realtor and said, "I like this place." A feeling had swept over me, and I knew I had found it. I was home. Soon, we set about restoring and decorating.

Our first major renovation was the kitchen. We decided to expand the existing, cavernous "galley" kitchen by combining it with what was a truly hideous 1950s addition to the house that we had come to call "the Florida room." This involved removing a wall—an original exterior wall. On the morning the carpenters were scheduled to begin demolition, I got cold feet. After all, we are supposed to regard owning an antique house as a responsibility, and one to be taken quite seriously. Were we doing the right thing by our old home?

Sensing my pensive mood, Suzanne sought to distract me. She read aloud from Haynes R. Mahoney's *Yarmouth's Proud Packets.* The evocative passage she chose had to do with the first owner of our house, Captain Ed Hallet, and Ed's friend and business partner, Elisha Doane. It was the 1830s, and Wharf Lane was known as Central Street, a busy avenue of commerce leading from the village to Central Wharf. Elisha was a prominent local citizen—a ship captain himself—who became the richest man in town, building ships, insuring vessels and owning a tavern, which still stands just west of the playground on the north side of Old King's Highway.

The mention of Elisha Doane rang a bell. Something drew me upstairs, where I took an antique mirror off the wall. I remembered the mirror was a purchase we made at the time we bought the house. The auctioneer we bought it from had said, "You know, you should keep this. It came from a Cape Cod house." It is a fairly humble object, but it is in its undisturbed, original condition, and it spoke to us. Now, as I turned the mirror over, I saw something I had either never noticed or had long forgotten, something that made the hair on the back of my neck stand up. There, on the backboard in bold chalk script was the name of the mirror's original owner: Elisha Doane. I brought it down to show Suzanne and said, "I think we are OK." I have never again asked myself, "Are we doing the right thing?" That question has been answered.

George Adams

For a number of years after we bought our house, our neighbor across the street was Martha White. Martha had been the librarian at the Yarmouth Port Library for a full half century, beginning in 1937. She had grown up in her house, which, like ours, was built in the third decade of the nineteenth century and had always been in her family. I loved sitting in her front parlor, listing to Martha tell stories of living here years ago. She related that Alice Hallet, last in the line of Hallets to live in Ed Hallet's house, had married a farmer named George Adams.

According to Martha White, George was quite a character. During Prohibition, he ran an illegal distillery in the barn that used to be located on the north side of the house. Martha's mother was fond of holding elegant tea parties on her lawn for her friends. During one such event, the ladies, who had been blissfully unaware of the goings-on across the lane, were scandalized when the Feds chose that day to raid the still!

Our house can claim a rich and varied history. Perhaps Ed's presence is not entirely alone here. Plaques commemorating Captains' Mile are affixed to Yarmouth Port homes that were owned by sea captains—and there are many of them. Ours is the only one with the finish peeling off of it. Coincidence? Or the mischievous work of the ghost of George Adams?

GHOSTS OF CENTER STREET

Center Street is a street with a rich history and interesting tales about those who once lived there. Ancient Cemetery, Cape Cod's second cemetery, is located on this street.

Historic figures of Yarmouth such as Squire Doane, Reverend Timothy Alden and Willie Bray were laid to rest here. Ancient Cemetery was the original location of the First Congregational Church, the first church of Yarmouth. Built in 1639, it enabled Yarmouth to be incorporated as a town.

Center Street is lined with old homes where sea captains and ministers once lived. According to some living there today, those who once lived on Center Street still make their presence known.

1 Center Street
Woman in White

At the corner of Center Street and Main Street is a lovely old home built in the mid-1800s. Today the house is operated as an inn. There have been ongoing rumors concerning incidents at the inn at 1 Center Street. Recently, one of the former owners of the inn stepped forward to recount what occurred during her tenure as innkeeper.

She cannot remember if she saw it first or perhaps it was a guest who had seen it. It happened as the busy season for tourists was beginning to wane. A guest came downstairs and remarked about the "presence" that she felt in the rear of the house. "Do you experience this often?" she asked. No one had mentioned it before, so the experience was a new one.

Number 1 Center Street, Yarmouth. The house is now an inn. Several strange stories have come from this location.

Not too long afterward, the innkeeper was at the foot of the back stairs. As she looked up to the upper hallway, she saw her. The apparition was a young woman dressed in a flowing white dress. The innkeeper just looked at the vision. She wasn't frightened; as a matter of fact, she had a rather good feeling about the entire experience.

It was late fall and the owners were away on vacation. They had asked a good friend to oversee the operation of the inn, as it was a rather slow season for guests. While they were away, the young woman appeared again at the back staircase. This made a memorable visit for the friend, who recounted her startling story to the owners upon their return.

It has been reported that the inn was once a property owned by Squire Doane when he was a young man. A young woman did die on this property, but who she was we do not know. She was, however, a guest in the room on the left at the top of the rear stairway.

A Little About 1 Center Street and Elisha Doane

This home was owned by the notorious squire Elisha Doane, Yarmouth's highly successful businessman and opportunist. The owner of many properties in Yarmouth, Squire Doane loaned 1 Center Street to the First Congregational Church for use as a parsonage. Reverend Packard lived there in 1858, and Reverend Dodge in 1880. When Squire Doane died, he left 1 Center Street to the church. Today, the house is privately owned and is operated as a lovely inn.

The squire owned Squire Doane's Tavern, a tavern for the gentry located at the corner of what are now Playground Road and Main Street. He also had businesses in shipping, shipbuilding and insurance. Squire Doane was known for taking advantage of any opportunity. It has even been rumored that he sold slaves on his front lawn. (This is typical of the stories told about him, but this one couldn't be true. In 1792, Elisha Doane was voted by town meeting to be allowed to settle in Yarmouth. Slavery had been outlawed in Massachusetts nine years earlier.) Although he was president of the Temperance Society, he often paid his employees their wages in rum. (For more on Elisha Doane, see the story of 57 Wharf Lane.)

15 Center Street

In the 1800s, the property at 1 Center Street included more land than it does today. After the property was subdivided, a house was built at 15 Center Street in 1958 behind the original house. Built as a private home, this house was soon sold to the First Congregational Church and was used for many years as a parsonage. It remained a parsonage until the 1980s, when it was sold by the church and once again became a private home.

When the Johnstons purchased the home in the early 1980s, they realized that the foundation needed repair. Work was progressing well, until Mr. Johnston reached the area between the garage and kitchen. As he began removing foundation stones from this area, a tremendous gust of cold air rushed out of the basement. Mr. Johnston found the incident strange, but thought no more of it.

The home remained in the Johnston family, and eventually Robyn, the Johnstons' daughter, raised her family there. When a baby girl was born, strange things began to happen. Kitchen lights were found on even though Robyn was sure she had turned them off. Basement chairs were rearranged, and some that had not been moved had indented cushions indicating that they had been used recently. While Robyn thought these things were strange, she did not believe in ghosts or believe that the house was haunted. As Robyn's daughter, Jessie, grew older, she also began to notice strange things and began to talk of them with her mother. Because of this, Robyn became more aware of what was happening in the house. Eventually, when Jessie was seven years old, Robyn could no longer ignore the strange things occurring in the house.

Both Robyn and Jessie continued to notice basement chairs being moved from where they had been placed. In April, they noticed a strong smell of cigar smoke in the house. This happened every April. When Jessie became old enough to go out on her own, she took a job and moved from the house. She found work at the inn at 1 Center Street, right next door. Living so close to home, she often stopped by to see her family.

In 2001, strange sounds were heard in the house at 15 Center Street. There were sounds of banging, doors slamming and glass breaking, and at times it sounded as if someone were running up and down the hall. These sounds always happened around 4:00 in the morning. Upon waking and going into the kitchen and living room, Robyn found everything in order. There was no physical evidence to explain what she had heard during the early morning hours.

Although Robyn did not hear these noises on a regular basis, she recalls that one time they continued for six weeks. Needless to say, Robyn was frightened. To this day, she sleeps with the lights on when she is alone in the house. However, leaving the lights on doesn't always help. Often she has awakened, sensing someone in the room. When she opens her eyes, no one is there.

Both Robyn and Jessie believe there is more than one ghost. They believe that one is a child. One night, when Jessie was staying at the house, both she and her mother awoke when their dog, Tucker, began acting strangely. Both saw the dog wagging his tail and looking down the hall toward the living room. They watched as he then ran to the living room and began playing with someone. He ran back and forth between the bedroom and the living room over and over again. The living room ghost was different from the others. It was playful, and Tucker seemed to enjoy its company.

Other ghosts that frequent this house are not so playful or friendly. One, a man, seems to be very angry. Once when Robyn and her husband, Jim, were asleep in their room, she awoke to the sound of loud banging. She thought someone was breaking into the house. Then she saw a figure enter the room and go to the side of the bed where Jim was sleeping. She watched as the figure tore what she perceived to be a piece of paper over him. After that, the figure moved to her side of the bed and then departed. All of this took place over the period of an hour. This ghost tears things, bangs about the house and even shakes the bed in which people are sleeping.

Family members have smelled scents in the house at inappropriate times. Sometimes during the summer, when the fireplace is not in use, there is a smell of a wood fire. Other times, they smell cigar smoke when no one is smoking. Once there was a smell of strong perfume coming from the bathroom, but no one had used perfume in that room. The family found this particularly strange, as previously there had been no indication of an unknown woman's presence in the house. Then, both Robyn and Jessie saw a young woman dressed in a blue gown in the bathroom. When they looked in the mirror, no one was present.

The eeriest incident of all occurred one evening during a dinner party. Everyone was seated at the table enjoying a lovely evening together, when suddenly the chandelier began to swing back and forth slowly. As the chandelier moved, one guest's water glass rose to eye level and tipped, spilling water on the table. Not surprisingly, this friend is no longer willing to visit 15 Center Street!

The family living in the house at 15 Center Street believes it is the land that is haunted and not the house itself. When gardening, they find old pottery and other things buried in the dirt. They believe that something unusual, perhaps even strange, happened on the land a very long time ago. Was it a burial ground? We may never know.

GHOSTS OF ANCIENT CEMETERY

Ancient Cemetery, the second oldest cemetery on the Cape, has been called the most active of all Cape cemeteries by some paranormal research societies. Why? Many speculate that it has to do with an event that took place in 1826.

The Moving of Graves

At the January 4, 1826 Yarmouth town meeting, it was "voted that all of the people of colour shall in the future, bury their dead in the Southeast corner of the burying yard [Ancient Cemetery]." The situation worsened when the town

> *voted that Thomas Greenough & all other people of colour be requested to remove their dead from the place where they are now deposited & bury them in the Southeast corner of the burying ground, as is to be laid out by the Selectmen for that purpose.*

Next, it was

> *voted that William Bray & Captain Joshua Eldridge be requested to call on Thomas Greenough & others, & request them to remove their dead to the Southeast corner of the burying yard, agreeable to the vote of this meeting.*

At that time, the term "people of colour" referred to both blacks and Native Americans who had been residents of Yarmouth.

Thomas Greenough and the others had very little time to carry out this task, even if they had agreed to do so. Frost in the ground during the first three months of the year gave them only a month to move all of the graves. They were unable to accomplish this awful task, and the town meeting appointed a committee to finish the job.

The town meeting on May 15, 1826, approved the following motion:

The southeastern corner of the Ancient Cemetery on Center Street, Yarmouth. This is the location to which the Native American graves were moved. Notice the absence of gravestones.

Voted that Captain Prince Matthews & Captain James Matthews be a committee appointed to remove the coloured people that are buried near to the wife of Sylvanus Studley and the daughter of William Bray, to some other part of the burying yard.

The committee never marked the new grave sites.

Why would William Bray, a respectable shipbuilder, get involved in something this distasteful? One can only speculate. It is believed that Sylvanus Studley may have been the primary force in having the graves moved. Studley's wife died in July 1825. Bray's daughter had died ten years earlier. Regardless, both William Bray and Sylvanus Studley were implicated, and their names will always be attached to this terrible deed.

Some say the ghosts you see at Ancient Cemetery are relatives of those whose graves were moved, searching for their loved ones. The southeast corner of the cemetery has very few markers in it, but it is filled with graves of blacks and Native Americans whose remains were moved by decree of that infamous Yarmouth town meeting. This incident was a sad indication of the treatment received by Native Americans and free blacks in the Northern "free" states. Unfortunately, it was not uncommon.

In December 2005, a tremendous windstorm struck Cape Cod, blowing down many trees. Ancient Cemetery suffered the loss of only one large tree. It was located near the graves of Hannah Studley and Frances Bray, and when it fell, it pointed in the direction of the relocated graves.

Bill Barnatt, a resident of Yarmouth who lives nearby, walked down to see the damage. The tree's roots had pulled up soil but no gravestones. In the soil, Bill found a white quartz arrowhead. It, too, was pointed toward the relocated graves.

Always Watching

Another gravesite, this one in the northeast corner of the cemetery, has its own story. This story is told by one of our researchers.

I was recently at a yard sale in my neighborhood. While talking with the owner of the property, we discussed the beauty of the area and how peaceful it was to live near Ancient Cemetery. She laughed, said it was certainly colorful and related her story.

It seems that a neighbor had died several years ago. Prior to her death, she had purchased a plot in the cemetery across the street that overlooked her home. The new owners, aware that she was buried across the street, sensed the presence of the woman. They felt they had to maintain the property as she had left it and they certainly sensed her disapproval when they made alterations that she didn't like. It is as if she were watching them, always tending to her beloved home.

The home has changed hands a few times since the woman's death. Each new homeowner has felt the scrutiny of the woman. They feel she is always watching, always vigilant.

The Curse

There is a gravestone not far from the maintenance shed on Ancient Way that contains a curse. It is not an old gravestone—just one person's anger with her neighbors carved into posterity. The curse reads:

> *May eternal damnation be*
> *upon those in whaling port*
> *who, without knowing me,*
> *have maliciously vilified me*
> *may the curse of god*
> *be upon them and theirs*

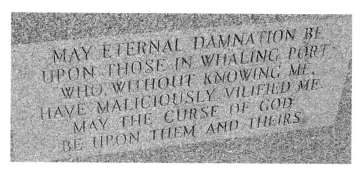

Not all legends are old. This curse in Ancient Cemetery dates from the 1980s.

Orbs

There are reports of orbs in Ancient Cemetery. Although not unusual for a cemetery, it is the amount of activity that sets this cemetery apart from others. Using electronic devices, paranormal investigators have searched the burial ground. According to their reports, there is an area located in the section of cemetery near Winter Street that has more orbs flying around than any other place in the cemetery or, for that matter, any other cemetery. The location is near another modern gravesite with a dark gravestone.

Paranormal orbs are spheres of energy not visible to the human eye, but which can be captured on film or digital recording devices such as today's digital cameras. They typically appear in areas where ghosts or other paranormal activities occur. Some believe orbs are the essence of a departed soul.

Cape Cod Superstitions

Cape Codders believed in several superstitions regarding ghosts at cemeteries. These include:

1) Carry a lump of bread in your pocket when walking in the dark. It will serve as an offering to ghosts.
2) If you see a ghost, walk around it nine times and it will disappear.

The best example of an orb that the editor has found. Fourteen-year-old Tyler Filka fell asleep in one of the captains' houses on Captains' Mile. This picture shows the orb very clearly. *Photo courtesy of Donna Cote.*

3) If you can't walk around it, crow like a rooster. The theory: ghosts don't wear watches and they will flee if they think daylight is coming.

4) When passing a graveyard or a house where someone has died, turn your pockets inside out. This will ensure that you don't bring ghosts home in your pockets.

5) Some believe that turning an article of clothing inside out while sleeping will make you safe from ghosts. Children often did this.

A third grader related to one of the historical society researchers that turning clothes inside out helped the Red Sox win their world championship in 2004. The Red Sox were down three games to none and behind in game four of the American League playoffs against the New York Yankees, when fans put on "rally caps" by turning their hats inside out—to drive away the "curse of the Bambino."

32 OLD CHURCH STREET
Eleanor's Home

This house was built by a one-armed Civil War veteran, Albert Taylor. He and his wife, a woman of Italian or Greek origin, lived in the house until their deaths. The property eventually passed to the Howes family. After World War II, the large barn at the back of the property was used to board horses. The road to it was lined with lavender bushes. One of the people to board a horse there was Irina Lutskya. She always came with a bodyguard, although the reason was never clear. Near the barn were two gravestones, presumably those of Albert Taylor and his wife. Where the stones and/or graves have been moved to is a mystery for another time.

Howes's wife was named Eleanor. She demanded that the place be spotless—neat as a pin. When Eleanor died, the cleaning standards deteriorated. One night, the family was sitting in the living room. Suddenly, the dog awoke with a start and immediately left the room. Soon, the hair on people's arms stood on end. After this happened a few times, the family thought they realized what was happening. At each incident, they would say, "Eleanor is back, checking on us."

Over the years, the house continued to deteriorate. When the current owners purchased it, some renovations had been completed, but much remained to be done. The house is now beautifully refinished, and sometimes visitors remark that they can smell a sweet aroma, even though no spray or incense has been used. It must be Eleanor telling them that she likes the way they are taking care of her house!

OTHER YARMOUTH VILLAGES

SOUTH YARMOUTH

Sections of South Yarmouth have been known by a variety of names. These include Middletown, Georgetown, Quaker Village, Indian Town and Bass River. Bass River, the site of one of the busiest seaports on Cape Cod, was the home to many an oceangoing sailing vessel.

Simpkins School
The Ghost in the Attic

Over the years, there have been numerous rumors about a ghost in the attic of the Simpkins School. Although no one we know of has actually reported a ghost, many believe one exists. The Simpkins School was built in 1932 and was used as the consolidated high school for Yarmouth and Dennis until the current high school was constructed. The building

The Simpkins School on Old Main Street, South Yarmouth. The rumors of a ghost in the attic date from pre–World War II.

was then converted to the Simpkins Elementary School. The town has since closed the school.

On March 30, 1995, an article in the *Yarmouth Register* briefly alluded to this ghost, but nothing more was ever written about it.

In compiling this collection of ghost stories, several members of the historical society interviewed people who were familiar with the building. They contacted teachers, cafeteria workers, former students and townspeople who had knowledge of the school. Most said they knew little or nothing about the ghost. Two remember having heard stories, but they couldn't recall the details.

The most interesting story was told by someone who graduated from the school more than fifty years ago. She remembered the story and thought it was either a teacher or administrator at the school who started the story of a ghost in the attic. According to her, the story's intent was to keep inquisitive younger students from sneaking up to this less-than-safe area that was off limits. But, the rumor may have made it an even more alluring challenge.

There was a school principal in the 1930s named Dyke Quackenbush who was a likely candidate for creating the rumor.

188 Old Main Street
The Crooked House

The house, built on James Pond in the 1600s was later moved to Old Main Street in the 1700s. The "Crooked House" burned in 1984 and was rebuilt by a subsequent owner.

The Indian Infirmity

During the course of its history, the house was once an infirmary for the last of the local Native Americans who were stricken by a smallpox epidemic.

Lucy Boston, one of the last Native Americans to live in Indian Town (South Yarmouth), married Judah Cato. They lived in a teepee near the corner of Old Main Street and Aiken Avenue. Lucy was the mother of Mary Dunn. Lore has it that Lucy didn't want to work at 188 Old Main Street because she saw spirits there. Could they have been the spirits of the smallpox victims?

The Ghost of John Stetson

John Sears, an eleventh-generation Yarmouth resident, relates his account of the Crooked House.

It was the late Ann Maxtone-Graham, a founder of the Historical Society of Old Yarmouth and the Yarmouth Library Association, who gave the house its name. She called it the Crooked House "because there wasn't anything straight about it."

The house eventually became the home of Sears's great-great-grandfather, Barnabas Sears. Barnabas had four sons and a daughter. The daughter married John Stetson. After she died, Stetson sold the home to the Taylor family, with the provision that he would have lifetime living accommodations. The Taylors built a cottage in the rear of the property for Stetson. One day he died, presumably overcome by smoke from a coal stove. But that wasn't the end of John Stetson—sightings of Stetson continued throughout the years.

Sears recalls that the Crooked House was always the talk of the town, and not just because of its unusual architecture. Everyone knew about the ghost of John Stetson. Other reported hauntings included window shades that moved up and down by themselves and closed windows that were found open in the morning.

Laurence Barber, in his book, *When South Yarmouth was Quaker Village*, chronicles a different version of the Dr. John Stetson story.

Dr. Stetson and his wife lived in the old Kelly/Pollard/Crooked House at 188 Old Main Street, where Elizabeth's mother had grown up. When Elizabeth died, the house was sold, with the stipulation that Dr. Stetson, then aged ninety-five, should stay there with kitchen privileges. The new owner wanted to use the building as his guesthouse, so he built a small cottage in back for Dr. Stetson.

However, Stetson soon died. Several years later, the main house was occupied by one of the owner's relatives. She noticed her dogs' fear when they approached the empty cottage, and asked her maid, who was newly arrived from Jamaica, what the reason could be.

The maid told her that the dogs were afraid of the man who lived in the cottage. The owner of the property, who was present, objected, stating that the cottage was vacant. The maid insisted that a man was living there. She had seen him frequently. She even described the man, to the consternation of the owner and his wife, for the description was that of Dr. John Stetson, who had died long before the maid had ever come to Yarmouth.

Into the Cellar

When local realtor Les Campbell was growing up in South Yarmouth, he never imagined how many ways he would "cross paths" with the mysterious Crooked House property. As children, Campbell and his friends would walk down Old Main Street on their way to the Simpkins School. "When you got to the [Crooked] house, you ran by it, because it was said to be haunted," he recalled.

Years later, as a realtor, he would not only sell the property to a new owner, but he would also have his own mystical encounter there. One of Campbell's clients was so intrigued by the house's reputation that she decided to buy it.

"It had a round Cape Cod cellar under the kitchen, used to store vegetables in the days before refrigeration," Campbell said.

While the new owner waited upstairs, Campbell went down into the cellar with a flashlight to look around. "Suddenly, the trapdoor closed and my flashlight went out." Campbell wasted no time scurrying up the stairs, only to find the new owner laughing.

The Crooked House at 188 Old Main Street, South Yarmouth. Ghosts from Native American times as well as the ghost of Dr. John Stetson lingered here until the building burned in 1984.

WEST YARMOUTH

Laurence Barber wrote a book about West Yarmouth and titled it *West Yarmouth—A Village Ignored*. This section of town was more rural than the others. After the Civil War, it became a destination for tourists, and development along its main road (Route 28) flourished. The following are stories from this area.

Family, Friend or a Guest From the Past
The Flapper

There is a fairly new home located in West Yarmouth near where the Englewood Hotel once stood. It is a quiet neighborhood close to the beach. In earlier days, when the hotel was new, the Englewood was a beehive of summer activity. The hotel is now gone, but the memories live on, and so do some of the people that once frolicked there.

A young family moved into this home several years ago. There was the young couple, their toddler and the young live-in babysitter who was a part-time bakery worker.

One evening after midnight, the husband adjourned to the master bedroom. As he entered, he was startled to see a woman in his room. She was standing in front of the dresser, looking into the mirror and brushing her hair. It was strange enough to see this person before him, but her attire was even more unusual. She was wearing a flapper-style clinging chemise. The hair she was brushing was a short bob, either very blonde or white. The young fellow was stunned by her appearance, and he watched as she casually groomed herself as if preparing to go out for the evening. Once finished, she disappeared.

Noisy Footsteps

This young couple would often watch television in the den so as not to disturb the babysitter who retired very early each evening. She worked the morning shift at the bakery.

It was a summer evening, and the young wife was watching television into the wee hours when she heard footsteps in the hallway. The steps came closer, but stopped near the bedroom. The babysitter also heard them. The footsteps were loud enough to wake her, and she was quite irritated with the couple for making so much noise. The noisy footsteps were heard frequently that summer, but there was never anyone there.

Interestingly, the family has had similar experiences elsewhere. Others have heard footsteps and felt a presence when visiting their home. Does the family experience periodic visits from long departed relatives? If so, who are they and who is the charming flapper? Is she someone's late aunt, or a reveler from the Englewood Hotel who is revisiting the haunts of her youth?

Strange Feelings
A Vacation Not to Remember

It was a perfect summer day in 1985 and the start of a one-week vacation on Cape Cod for me and Susie, my eleven-year-old daughter. I had answered an ad in a Boston paper for a rental cottage in West Yarmouth. The one-and-a-half-hour ride from our home in Stoneham went smoothly. As soon as we reached the Cape, we proceeded to study a road map to find our way to West Yarmouth.

I recall driving around Hyannis for several minutes, when, suddenly, Susie began to sing "Follow the Yellow Brick Road" from *The Wizard of Oz*. Just as we rounded a bend, from out of nowhere a street sign appeared that read: "Yellow Brick Road." We were both amazed, as we had had no idea that such a road existed.

The real fun began after we found our rental house. It was within short walking distance to Lewis Bay Harbor. We arrived just before noon on a Saturday. There was a car parked out front, and a man was in the process of loading it. I assumed it was the prior renter. That meant we would have to return later to unpack our things.

As we drove a little farther down the road, we came to a small public beach overlooking the harbor. The salt water and sandy beach were a welcome sight after the long drive. We took full advantage of the opportunity for some fun, sun and relaxation.

About mid-afternoon, we headed back to the cottage, which now appeared to be vacant. It struck me as an odd little house, almost too tall for its width and painted blue. The place looked somewhat quaint, as the stairs that led to the upper bedrooms were steep and narrow, and the furnishings were from a bygone era. But the cottage was clean and neat.

Upon exploring the yard, Susie immediately spotted a large bush and, delighted, set to the task of picking its ripe berries. I decided to take a shower in the downstairs bathroom, which was so narrow that scarcely one person could fit in there at a time. My daughter slipped inside while I was showering, saying that she just wanted to be there with me. This seemed unusual for her, but I didn't mind and didn't think much of it at the time.

Later that evening, while we were sitting in the living room, Sue noticed an old bookcase and pulled out a book to read. From between its pages fell seven dollars (a stroke of luck?).

In writing this story, I have recently questioned my daughter about her recollection of the events that took place in the cottage. She insists that she found six dollars in a Bible at the place where it describes "666, the mark of the beast." If she had mentioned it at the time, neither one of us would have understood the ramifications until much later.

At about 9:00 p.m., my daughter and I went upstairs to prepare for bed. We had decided to sleep together in the larger of the two bedrooms, which had a double bed. The other room contained a baby's highchair that had been painted black and a single bed.

In the larger bedroom, there was a picture on the wall of one of those 1950s babies with the enormous eyes. My daughter, who now knows antiques, tells me it was a Margaret Keene "Pop Art" of the 1960s.

As I was undressing, Sue suddenly felt frightened, stating something was watching us from a distance. She urged me to hurry—that we had better get out of the house—soon! In less than five minutes, she went from acting fearful to becoming downright hysterical as she pleaded with me to HURRY! Something was watching us, and getting closer by the minute.

I was afraid for her, but otherwise I felt nothing unusual, nor did I feel nervous about being there. I realized that my eleven-year-old daughter was in earnest and in such a panic that it was imperative for us to leave the premises immediately. I even suggested that she go and wait for me in the car (in the pitch dark) if she preferred—which, in fact, she did, while I gathered some last-minute belongings to take with us.

That night we drove to my sister's home in West Harwich. The next morning, Susie, my sister and I went back to West Yarmouth to collect the rest of our belongings. We did not attempt to stay in the rented house for the remainder of our visit to Cape Cod.

My daughter recently told me that she was surprised not to feel any fear or anxiety while at the cottage that day. Even as a child, Susie has always been a strongly independent and fearless individual; in fact, I don't know anyone who is more intrepid than she! Therefore, I have never doubted that there was something truly disturbing about that cottage in West Yarmouth. As she recently put it, describing her feelings at the time, it was as though we were in "mortal danger." She also states that she "felt silly to be scared," that "it didn't make sense" and she "hadn't wanted to admit that she was so scared."

Other Cape Cod Towns

Dennis

The Cape Playhouse
Footsteps on Sunday

For years, Helen Pond and Herbert Senn created and installed the sets for the summer playhouse. Both Helen and Herbert were world-renowned set designers. During a thirty-eight-year period, they designed more than 350 sets for the playhouse.

Helen and Herbert were often at the playhouse late on Sunday evenings preparing the sets for the next production. After everyone had left, and while applying the finishing touches on the new set, they would hear someone walking in high heels on the wooden floor. The footsteps always came from the area where the audience seats are located. This would only occur late on a Sunday evening. Although they heard the footsteps, they never saw anything or anyone.

The Cape Playhouse, Dennis. This is the oldest continually operating summer theatre in New England. Gertrude Lawrence was

very active here, both as an actress and owner. Some believe her spirit is still present.

Neither Helen nor Herbert had ever met Gertrude Lawrence, a leading star and wife of the playhouse founder, but both believed the footsteps had to be hers. They believed Gertrude was just checking to make sure that the sets were perfect. Helen and Herbert would laugh about it, but they never mentioned the footsteps to anyone just in case someone was playing a trick on them.

Herbert died in 2003. No one has come forward to say they were the source of the footsteps. Helen feels even more certain that it was the ghost of Gertrude Lawrence. While they had met and worked with many famous actors and actresses over the years, only Gertrude Lawrence would have been wearing high heels that late on a Sunday evening.

Superstitions

There is a superstition that states: if an emptied theatre is left completely dark, a ghost will take up residence. The belief is that ghosts of past actors and actresses will return to the stage to live out their glory moments. To prevent this, one must leave a single light burning at center stage after everyone has left the theatre.

There is another version in which some believe a single light is traditionally left on at center stage to light the way for the ghosts of past actors and actresses.

A Little About Helen and Herbert

Helen Pond and Herbert Senn were world renowned for their set designs. Both had been designing sets since they first met at the Columbia Graduate School for Theater Arts. Over the years, they designed sets for shows on Broadway, as well as in England and Russia, and produced sets for the Opera Company of Boston. The Cape Museum of Fine Arts featured an exhibit on models of their sets made for the Opera Company. Among the many awards they received for their designs was the Elliot Norton Award for outstanding theatre design in Boston. Their most famous was the set they created for *The Nutcracker* in Boston. What most don't know is that the set was built in their workshop on Higgins Crowell Road in West Yarmouth. They are best known locally for their work and design of the sets used at the Cape Playhouse in Dennis between 1956 and 1994.

Helen and Herbert's home is a converted church in the village of Yarmouth Port. Today, 17 Church Street, which was completely redecorated by them, remains a lasting memory to the artistry of these two extremely gifted people. Even at the "church," their care is obvious. The original pews are numbered and stored in the attic. The house could be converted back when and if the time should be right. People who have attended concerts or receptions at their home know just how talented both Helen and Herbert were. The memories visibly remain there, and there is no need for ghosts to enhance history.

Strawberry Hill on Church Street. This former Universalist/Unitarian church was renovated and converted into a private home by world-renowned set designers Helen Pond and the late Herbert Senn.

BARNSTABLE

4312 Old King's Highway
The John Gorham House

The house was built in the 1670s and is affectionately known as the Gorham House. John Gorham was obviously pleased with the house, for it has long been mentioned that the house is filled with pleasant ghosts.

Tales of Past Inhabitants

The current owner, Rick Jones, doesn't believe the stories, but he knew that many of its former residents had died in the house, some of unknown causes. More than once he has felt the presence of someone when no other person was around.

Only once has he seen something unusual—a reflection in a mirror of a young woman, dressed in what he assumed to be eighteenth-century clothing that was light and airy. He saw only the reflection, nothing more.

Several people have actually had contact with John Gorham or another spirit. A woman who was visiting saw John Gorham sitting on a couch facing the fireplace. When she spoke to him, he disappeared.

Jack Braginton-Smith's daughter, Heather, a Cape Cod artist, used to visit the property regularly. She preferred to come during the day, because at night, with the fireplace going and candles lit, Heather experienced a very eerie feeling. Others noted that she would speak in different "tongues."

Barbara Breidenbach related an especially unusual event that occurred a number of years ago. She was seated on the couch in the living room; the room was lit by the fireplace and a small light. Suddenly, Barbara noticed a hand on the back of the couch. It was an older woman's hand, complete with polished fingernails. Her dress had long sleeves and was made of deep purple velvet. There were lace cuffs. On her finger was an old amethyst ring. When Barbara turned to look, the hand disappeared.

No one knows who the woman might have been. Could it have been John Gorham's wife? He was certainly wealthy enough to afford the clothing and ring. Perhaps it was one of the later Gorham wives.

Barbara had another experience that she feels involved John Gorham. She was sleeping on a sofa in the living room. As she awakened, she saw "old English" writing being created on a blank portion of the wall. The writing said, "Jonathan wants to meet you in the garden." After she read it, the writing disappeared.

She decided not to wander out to the garden. The writing had scared her and she didn't want to leave—or go back to sleep. No one has been able to explain why the name Jonathan was used. Both Gorham and his son were named John. Perhaps if she wasn't so unnerved, she might have been able to find out who Jonathan was. She didn't realize at the time that the ghosts in this house were friendly and meant no harm.

Everyone who visits the house notices that it seems to exude a very warm and pleasant feeling. While Rick Jones still says he doesn't believe in ghosts, he can't explain what others have seen or felt. Rick is quick to point out that none of the interactions with his guests have been anything but pleasant.

An Unusual Visit

The following stories are told by Chris Moriarty, Rick's nephew.

Number 4312 Old King's Highway, Barnstable. This building is considered by some to be the Mecca for shore whaling on Cape Cod. Some of the ghosts from this building go back to shore-whaling days.

"I do believe in spooks, I do believe in spooks, I do I do I do I do I do believe in spooks," was what the cowardly lion muttered to himself, and just like him, I softly spoke the same words while lying in bed at age sixteen. I was visiting my uncle at the old Gorham House on Cape Cod, Massachusetts. I had been through both an ethereal and terrifying day of pranks and human-like mirages, and I wanted to get a sound sleep without completely freaking out. Well, that's exactly what I got, the most amazing and deepest sleep I can ever recall. I had no memory of any dreams and woke up with my body in the exact same horizontal position with my hands folded neatly across my chest.

Throughout the Easter weekend, while visiting my uncle Rick with his mother, my grandmother, and his sister, my mother, I had a most unique experience in body, mind and spirit. There can be only one explanation for this most unusual and memorable of my life's experiences—the late John Gorham.

The first sign that there was something fishy going appeared when I returned from wandering outside in the gardens and came into the living room. I heard someone walking up the stairs and called out thinking it was my grandma, as the footsteps sounded very slow and she moved in such a manner. When I went to the front stairway, not only was my grandmother not there, but also the entire house was empty. The three of them had taken a drive somewhere, perhaps to the Christmas Tree Shop.

Immediately, a chill ran through me, starting at my midsection and spreading in opposite directions to my head and the soles of my feet. What had just happened? I was momentarily petrified. I regained my senses and took a quick walk out the front door and onto the lawn. I turned to look up at the windows. It was at this moment that I knew there was something beyond normal happening at the old Gorham House. There was also something paranormal drifting through the place, and this proved to be just the beginning.

When my family returned, I told my uncle what had happened. He joked, "Oh, that's probably John." I pushed for more information, but he had nothing further to give me other than allowing my imagination to run wild—and it did.

There was another incident the same day. Something caused the lids of pots, jars or other vessels to jump off their resting place, only to clink back down in place, startling me. To me, the phenomenon was as shocking and intriguing as a Mexican jumping bean. Perhaps I became hypersensitive, or some might even say paranoid, at the strange things that were happening in rapid succession. But the event that played out later that night was the one that caused me to pray both out loud and to myself as I tried to drift off to sleep.

We were all sitting by a fireplace in the living room, the same fireplace that has a secret passageway where slaves were hidden from their Southern pursuers. I beheld something that to this day I have never experienced again. As we enjoyed quiet conversation, with the adults sipping cocktails, an apparition walked into the room slowly. Time seemed to stand still for me. Out of the corner of my eye, I watched in awe as a short, male figure came near to share in our good spirits.

I could sense in his presence his approval of our family celebration. He was dressed in a long, dark gray coat that went almost to the floor and buttoned all the way to below the knees. Because of the length, I had no idea what was underneath. He moved slowly, yet purposefully, to be close to our family. I again could sense his approval of our sharing togetherness as a family. As soon as things started to speed back up to reality, he was gone. He did not turn around, but simply vanished like a cartoonist's animation cell that had run its course.

I asked if anyone had seen or experienced anything out of the ordinary, to which they asked what I was talking about. It was later that night, after talking to my grandmother, that I experienced the strangest thing of all. Before going to bed, I told my grandmother how scared I was. She told me to talk to the spirit and tell him how scared I was. As I was lying in my bed, I spoke out loud about my fears. I closed my eyes with my hands across my chest and fell asleep. When I awoke the next morning, I was in the exact same position.

Several years later, I returned to my uncle's home this time with a friend. My uncle was away, so we had this beautiful old house to ourselves. I had gone into my uncle's room to find a T-shirt to borrow, and helped myself to a green one with white trim that was soft and very comfortable. In retrospect, it was probably one of my uncle's favorite comfortable shirts. It was a hot night, and the shirt came off. Instead of folding it neatly, I tossed it on the floor at the foot of the bed.

When I awoke several hours later, I thought I would go downstairs to start on some breakfast. I went to the foot of the bed to grab the T-shirt, only to find it was not there. I looked under the bed and around the room. The shirt was nowhere to be found. As I was searching, I questioned my friend as to the whereabouts of the shirt. She knew nothing about it.

I don't exactly know why I did what I did next. I went back into my uncle's room and went over to the bureau from which I had taken the shirt. I opened the drawer and there, folded neatly on the top, was the green T-shirt. There really is no reasonable explanation for this. Could it have been the spirits looking out for my uncle's belongings while he was away?

A Little About John Gorham and Shore Whaling

John Gorham was the man most responsible for bringing order to the shore whaling industry. The whalers struggled to find a way to hunt right whales during the winter. In these months the right whales would come close enough to shore for whalers to give chase from shore-launched boats. The men, using twenty-foot-long rowboats, struggled to capture their prey. Gorham brought in a famous Dutch whaler, Jacobus Loper, to teach a standard way to row. This greatly increased the number of whales the boats captured.

If there was a Mecca for the whaling industry during the early times in America, this would have been the place.

The Crocker Tavern
Jack Braginton-Smith's Ghost Experience

Jack Braginton-Smith was a curmudgeon and Cape Cod legend who owned Jack's Outback in Yarmouth Port for a number of years. Jack was an outstanding historian and collector of historic memorabilia. He wrote many wonderful articles and two books about the Cape. Jack's experience with a ghost came before he took up residence above his restaurant. Before he died in July 2005, he had related his incident with a ghost to many people, including fellow writer and friend Duncan Oliver. This incident is just one of the many ghost stories related to the Crocker Tavern in Barnstable Village.

In the early 1980s, Jack was living in a room on the second floor at the Crocker Tavern. One night, while in bed and alone in the house, he heard footsteps coming up the stairs. Jack knew he had locked the door, was alone and no one else was expected.

Because the door to his room was closed, he couldn't see into the stairway area. Should he pretend he wasn't there, or walk over to the door and open it? Jack said he never thought that pulling a sheet over his head would offer any real protection. So, dressed only in undershorts and a T-shirt, Jack chose the latter.

The Crocker Tavern, Barnstable. Famous for a major encounter between Patriots and Tories during the Revolutionary War, lots of spirits have been encountered here.

With some trepidation, he went to the bedroom door and asked who was there. At that point, the footsteps stopped. Jack opened the door and looked down the stairs, but he saw no one. He decided he had better check the rest of the house, so he turned on lights and started looking, still in his half-dressed state. He heard absolutely nothing and did not find anyone in the house. He returned to his room. All remained quiet.

Oliver asked him how well he slept the rest of the night. His comment is not printable. When asked who he thought the ghost was, his reply was a typical Jackism: "For Chri-sakes Oliver, when you're standing there in your undershorts and just a little nervous, you don't ask the ghost his name."

James Hathaway's Sister

James Hathaway lived in both Yarmouth and Barnstable and was a staunch believer in witchcraft and its magical powers. He came from a family of strong men, one of whom could lift a full rum barrel and drink from the bunghole. The Hathaways lived in a secluded spot, some distance from neighbors. Some believe this had an influence on their character, causing eccentricity. Hathaway, when accused of embezzlement by a sister, disappeared suddenly. It was thought that he had drowned in the bay, and although they looked for him, fired guns, dragged sweeps and poured oil on the water, his body was not found.

Twenty-one years later, he returned to his wife and home. The sister who had accused him of embezzlement was a firm believer in witchcraft, and many wondered if she had bewitched him. She maintained that her brother ran away because he couldn't stand his wife and had only returned after the money ran out.

While a close-knit family they weren't, they were typical in their belief that witchcraft could be the cause of almost anything.

Robert the Scot

The ghost of "Robert the Scot" is known to travel Cape towns in a quest to clear his name.

Robert's real name was Robert Marshall. He was the indentured servant of Captain Matthew Fuller, a doctor from Barnstable. He assisted Dr. Fuller on his rounds as he treated people on Cape Cod. The doctor even treated the governor, Thomas Hinckley. Many considered Robert to be very strange—some even called him a madman.

Fuller was considered a rich man. When he died in 1678, his inventory listed "pearls, precious stones, and diamonds, at a guess 200 pounds." Sometime later, all of the valuables disappeared. Since Robert was always at his master's side, he became the prime suspect.

However, there was no proof, and Robert was never charged with the crime. Not satisfied, and with the valuables still missing, Robert threw himself into a search to locate them. As he played his bagpipes, he searched every likely and unlikely spot. He looked wherever Dr. Fuller had treated patients, including the neighboring towns of Yarmouth and Sandwich.

Some said his grief was so great that he was unable to swallow and he died of starvation. Robert Marshall was buried in a shallow grave on Scorton Hill. Afterward, people swore they could hear Robert playing his bagpipes as he continued his search.

Even today, especially on a windy day, there are reports of people hearing bagpipes. When will the bagpipes stop playing their song? Only when the valuables are found and Robert the Scot is cleared of suspicion. Then he will be able to forever sleep in peace.

SANDWICH

A Different Taste in Music

A funeral director in Sandwich had an interesting experience while renovating the funeral home. He and his son were remodeling the powder rooms in the oldest wing of the building. They had worked late into the night until just before dawn.

The undertaker sent his son out to get coffee and donuts. While the son was out, the funeral director continued to work on his project with the radio blaring rock music.

When the son returned, they took a break. As they were drinking their coffee, they heard the breaker in the electrical panel click. The power went out in their work area, cutting out the lights and the radio. Within minutes, they heard the breaker click again, and the power was restored.

When the radio came back on, there was soft, soothing classical music. A strong smell of heavy perfume wafted through the air. The men knew they were alone in the building. They became unsettled by the strange happenings and left.

The father and son are still puzzled by their early morning visitor. They have concluded that it was an older woman who preferred exotic, musky perfume and who had discriminating taste in music. Did she once live in the home or was she just a visitor passing through?

An Engaging Family
A Child Playing—Sandwich

There is a charming antique home in Sandwich that was once owned by Bob and his family. It was the type of Cape with the round Cape Cod basement. It was a pretty house, and the family was quite happy there.

Sometimes Bob and his wife would hear a child crying outside the house. Thinking it was one of their own, they would run outside to comfort the child, but there was never anyone there.

Other times, Bob and his wife would hear a child's footsteps coming in through the door and running 'round and 'round the kitchen. They heard giggles, or the child's voice chattering away, and out the door it would run.

Then, tragedy struck. The home was struck by lightning. Bob and his family were forced to move out of their home.

They moved into another home in a nearby town. Bob and his wife often wonder if the family that now occupies the Sandwich home is still visited by the giggly child.

A Hood-Cloaked Spirit—Hyannis

Bob and his family eventually settled in Hyannis. If their experience in their Sandwich home was cheerful, their new house was a bit more eerie. There was a dark spirit in the Hyannis house that was not always welcomed. He was dressed in a black hood, and he would float down the stairway that led from the bedrooms and disappear when he reached the bottom.

This spirit was a thief. Bob's wife complained that someone was taking her jewelry from her jewelry box. Her valuable pieces would disappear for weeks or even months at a time. Then the pieces would reappear rather dramatically. For instance, a necklace would drop from the ceiling onto the living room floor in front of them as they watched television. There was no one else in the house, nor were there any visible means of a hiding place in the ceiling. This happened several times.

One day, Bob was startled as he left the room and walked toward the stairway. Sitting on the bottom step was the hooded specter, holding his head in his hands as if he were troubled. When he looked up at Bob, there was no face.

There is no explanation as to who this pathetic figure was. Did he once live in this home? Why was he missing his face? No one really knows.

Inns, Bed-and-Breakfasts and Restaurants

Inns and bed-and-breakfast establishments have long been a part of Cape Cod's hospitality. While none of the stories are from the colonial period, some of the occurrences can be tracked back to that time in our history. This is just a sampling of stories that have taken place at various inns and bed-and-breakfasts.

The Colonial House Inn

It is only fitting to begin this chapter with the Colonial House Inn. It has been the center of attention for ghost stories for nearly thirty years. On several different occasions, paranormal societies and ghost busters have visited the inn to survey the property, the most recent occasion being in the spring of 2006. Some believe this building may well have more paranormal activity than any other house on Cape Cod!

Captain Joseph Eldridge lived here as early as 1804. He and his wife had nine children, four of whom died before reaching the age of one. When the captain died in 1856, he left the house to his youngest child, Azariah. Not following in his father's footsteps, Azariah became a doctor. Azariah and his wife, Ellen, had one child, who died at a young age. The child was buried in Connecticut, where Ellen was raised. Both Azariah and Ellen suffered from ill health, and when he died, she was unable to attend his funeral. Having no heir, she left the house to the First Congregational Church.

Since that time, the house has been owned by a number of different families. It had been used as a restaurant and then stood vacant for a number of years prior to Mac Perna purchasing the property in 1979.

Perna converted the structure into the current Colonial House Inn. It is from this period that we have most of the reported ghost sightings. Perna, who doesn't believe in ghosts, has asked guests who experienced unusual occurrences to write down their experiences. While he won't share those writings, he does say the same rooms have eerily similar experiences.

Guests' Stories

In the main house, there is a room where guests have reported hearing a baby cry. This is the room where at least one baby died when the home was owned by the Eldridges. In another room, a rocking chair sometimes turns during

A modern view of the Colonial House Inn. Many of the rooms where ghosts have been observed are visible in this photograph.

the night to face a blank wall. The wall that the rocker turns to face used to have a window in it. Different rocking chairs have been placed in the room with the same outcome—the rocking chair would always turn to face the ghost window.

A Cape Cod superstition seems to relate to this location as it pertains to the rocking chair. The superstition states that if you get up from a rocking chair and it is still rocking, it invites spirits to come into the house and sit in the chair.

Ghost noises are also heard in the attached carriage house. In one room, the sound of a boy crying is sometimes heard. This room used to house the stableboys. One stableboy reportedly hanged himself there. In another room, one sometimes hears the sounds of horses. The room was a former stall for the carriage horses.

Mac Perna, the innkeeper, received this email, dated July 4, 2006, from a guest:

> *Dear Mr. Perna, Recently we stayed at your inn. We only lasted 2 nights due to the ghosts that bothered us. When we booked our reservation we did not know it was haunted. My husband is much attuned to spirits, his mom was a medium. He saw a lady in white when we first arrived. The radio went on at midnight and the topper was at 3:30 a.m. when we were awakened by a blood curdling scream. The following night we left the light on all night and did not sleep one wink. I did mention this to the woman who works evenings and that's how we found out the inn was haunted. The staff and you are very nice, and the food was excellent, but I would never stay there again or recommend this inn to anyone unless they loved ghosts.*

Past Owner's Story

Elizabeth Embler, a daughter of one of the former owners wrote the following:

These two incidents happened when I was probably about ten years old, around 1970. We lived on Route 6A and ran an inn renting the rooms out during the summer months. As a result, we used different rooms in the house during the summer and winter. In summertime we would sleep in the back part of the house. I always looked forward to winter because I could pick a different room in which to sleep. I always wanted to try a new room. Room number eight on the third floor was my choice on this particular occasion. The numbering of the rooms may be quite different now.

I remember that I was lying in my bed in room number eight. Straight ahead was a window and there was another window to my right. I slept, but was awakened in the night. This had happened before when guests would come into my room mistaking it for theirs. But this time it was different. There was a man standing at the foot of my bed. He was wearing a brimmed hat, and he wore clothes from another time—yet I could tell he was a young man.

He was facing away from me with his arms folded. I watched him as he first looked out one window and then he turned and looked out of the other. I wanted to turn the light on, but I was afraid to. He did not speak to or look at me. For some reason, I knew it was not a real person. He was not someone I could talk to. It was more like a shadow than a real person. I could not identify his features. He stood there for what seemed like ten minutes, maybe fewer, and then he was gone. It did not happen again.

Another time I was sleeping on the third floor in the back of the house when I was awakened by a clock ticking loudly in the room. I was startled, for there was no clock in the room. I remember thinking, "There it is again, something in the room with me." I knew it was not a dream, for I had been fully awakened by the ticking of the clock.

Elizabeth was asked if she told anyone about these two instances. She can't remember if she told her mother at the time or not.

Paranormal Investigation—Sandra Richard

Sandra Richard, a psychic/medium and member of the International Ghost Hunters Society with eighteen years of experience, visited the Colonial House Inn during the spring of 2006. In her letter to innkeeper Mac Perna on June 15, 2006, she wrote:

> *Here are the pictures we talked about. One has an orb on the floor in front of the computer room door. The last has a good size but faint one toward the left corner of the door. Please feel free to use these any way you wish. I would appreciate it if you would use my name with them.*

Sandra Richard teaches classes on metaphysics, including the subject, "What are orbs?"

Some believe paranormal orbs are spheres of energy from the soul of a departed person. These orbs will contain the essences of the person, complete with their intelligence, emotions and personality. It is possible for a single orb to be composed of more than one soul. When its spirited energy is released, multiple orbs will flow forth from the single orb.

SERT Investigation

A paranormal detection team called SERT (Spirit Encounter Research Team) visited the Colonial House Inn during the spring of 2006. Before they arrived, the owner took down all pictures and documents that might have given the researchers clues. Only after they presented their findings did he share the pictures and documents with them.

In an email to the innkeeper on July 10, 2006, Reverend Richard Boisvere reported the following:

> *It is extremely important to note that, at no time, did I or any other member of the team feel threatened in any way. All personal experiences reported were described as "playful," "mischievous," and/or "friendly." Now to the investigation, throughout which, virtually all members of the team reported personal experiences. These experiences included, but were not limited to, sensations of being touched, (lady members of [the] team near dance floor) (male members near a room) being pinched, poked, and grabbed by unseen hands.*
>
> *As far as physical evidence is concerned, some EVPs or "electronic voice phenomena" were recorded. In one instance,*

when an audio recording device was placed in the Widow's Watch, children's voices and the sound of footsteps running up and down the stairs were clearly heard. This recording was made at approximately 1:45 a.m. when the building was quite silent. Once again the playful nature of the atmosphere remained. Later, in the same stairwell, a child's voice can be heard whispering very close to a hand-held microphone. "Hello" is the only word spoken. Explanations for such phenomena range from paranormal, to radio wave interference, to outright hoaxing—the latter of which, I can assure you is not the case.

These recordings will be transferred to a disk for our own records, but will also be available to you upon request, and eventually on our website for public scrutiny. Unfortunately, although our remote video equipment did pick up a rather interesting event, whereas dozens of "orbs" were seen swirling around an investigator, the equipment was, for unknown reasons, unable to record the event.

As for my own experiences, keep in mind that as a medium, much of what I experienced would still have been so even if there were never any reports of paranormal activity at this location.

While in the yard I encountered the spirit of a woman who graciously introduced herself as Mrs. Clarke, a name which was later substantiated by a document on the wall of one of the function rooms. (The innkeeper had removed all of *these documents before the team's arrival, replacing them only after the report.) I also felt the presence of a young gentleman who gave his name only as David. This man seems to have some connection to the development of the property. This name was also seen to be on a document in the lounge area dated 1812. A frail woman and a gentleman who was a physician were among the other entities I encountered, but once again, at no time did I feel the presence of anything but positive intent during these communications.*

I believe I speak for the entire team when I state we look forward to hearing from you and that, if you or anyone you know is ever in need of our services, please feel free to contact me or any member of the SERT family.

Additional Investigation

The Cape and Islands Paranormal Society, proponents of electronic voice phenomena, have electronically surveyed the Colonial House Inn. Their website lists their findings. These include apparitions, sounds and moving objects.

OLD YARMOUTH INN
Ghost or Freed Slaves?

The Old Yarmouth Inn has been a tavern since the 1690s. Local lore has it that Goodie Hallet, the poor lass who fell in love with the pirate Sam (Black) Bellamy, father of her child, was a tavern maid there. Unfortunately, there are no records supporting this wonderful story.

The current owners purchased the inn in 1996. The inn's website chronicles some ghostly incidents.

> *We suspect that there is really more than one ghost. The ghost(s) are not malicious or scary; rather he/she/they are mischievous and possess a good sense of humor.*

While not believers, the owners do say that strange things have happened. One morning, when Sheila's (one of the owners) sister went to the kitchen to make coffee, the mixer turned itself on.

The owners have had wineglasses fall from a secure rack and break and ashtrays rearrange themselves along the bar after being stacked. Could these be the quirks of an old house or, better yet, a ghost?

A 1920s postcard of Old Yarmouth Inn, 223 Old King's Highway, Yarmouth Port. The inn has had many stories of ghosts over the years.

Their website gives some of the inn's history as well, making it a very interesting read. One notation includes an anecdote from Althea Thompson, whose family owned the inn when it was a boardinghouse. She played in the attic and found a secret door that led to an unknown room. The website ponders whether the room might have held fugitive slaves who were escaping north on the underground railroad. Might "the ghost(s) be recently freed slave(s) seeking shelter en route to a safer life?"

The Cape and Islands Paranormal Research Society has electronically surveyed the Old Yarmouth Inn. Their website www.caiprs.com lists their findings, including sounds and moving objects.

The Red Rose Inn — Englewood Beach
The Spirit of Rose

On June 6, 2006, an article appeared in the *Cape Cod Times* that drew the attention of researchers from the historical society. The article featured the Red Rose Inn and the new owners, a mother/daughter team that had purchased the property in 2004. The Red Rose Inn is located at the end of Berry Avenue on Englewood Beach in Yarmouth.

The inn had been built as a private residence in the 1880s, at the time the area was first being developed. By 1902, the Englewood Beach area was under full development. The area's heydays were from the early 1900s through the 1930s.

Destruction caused by the hurricane of 1944 added to the already depressed conditions of the beach area. After World War II, the property was purchased by Red and Rose Rosenborough, who founded the inn (thus the name Red Rose Inn).

Red and Rose ran the inn until 1991. At which time they passed ownership to their grandson, Rick. Rick continued the family tradition until 2004, when he sold it to the current owners. Although the inn is no longer owned by the family, many believe Rose is still overseeing the property.

Rose loved hats. Part of her collection still remains at the inn. It is because of these hats that some feel Rose is forever present. Ruth, one of the owners, said they plan to redecorate one of the downstairs bathrooms and put some of Rose's pillbox hats on display.

Why there? Because it is obvious to many of the guests that Rose has never given up her feelings of ownership. Several "regulars" admitted to having seen a ghost in the hallway near the bathrooms. Others had felt a "presence." All believed it was Rose, although no one ever stated if she was wearing one of her hats. Grandson and former owner Rick Wilkey mentioned that he, too, had felt a presence.

Rose's favorite table was table number one, where she could look out over the beach. Seated behind this table, Rose could look both east and south toward Englewood Beach. Table number one is easy to identify, as it is the only circular table in the dining area. If you aren't lucky enough to sit there, perhaps you'll be seated at a table where Lincoln Filene or Elizabeth Taylor and Michael Todd once dined.

A Little History on the Englewood Beach Area

In 1902, the area started to develop into one of the town's premier tourist attractions. The Hotel Englewood opened nearby with twenty-five rooms. Four years later, the Englewood added a new wing. By 1920, electricity had been installed and another large new wing was added. Simeon P. Lewis even built a nine-hole golf course near the hotel.

The 1944 hurricane wreaked havoc on the house, destroying several nearby buildings, including the former Englewood Casino, then known as the Windmill Tearoom. The Englewood Hotel survived the hurricane, but couldn't survive changes in tourism. In January 1962, on a night so cold that water froze in the hoses, the hotel caught fire.

An aerial view of the Englewood Hotel in West Yarmouth, complete with horse stalls in the rear. The area has become highly developed since the time of this photograph.

When Red and Rose Rosenborough bought their property and started the inn, the area had begun a slow comeback. The Rosenboroughs began by selling food to those enjoying the beach, including hot dogs and hamburgers, ice cream and "tonic." These were purchased from a window in the kitchen area, so sand wouldn't be tracked into the inn. Today, the inn has a full menu served in the ocean-view dining room.

LIBERTY HILL INN
The Case of a Missing Leg

Although there are no paranormal happenings currently associated with the Liberty Hill Inn, there is a mystery that to this day has not been solved. The inn has a rich and historic past. Ezekiel Hallet, a well-known shipowner, along with a workforce of shipwrights, constructed the house. Two liberty poles were erected in the town of Yarmouth before and during the American Revolutionary War. The inn was constructed on one of the sites.

The house was converted to a bed-and-breakfast after World War II. In 1983, the owners initiated a major reconstruction project. During the rehabilitation, there was an eerie discovery—a human leg was found in the wall of the third story. The Yarmouth Police ordered the owner to halt the renovation immediately and started an investigation.

In 1983, at the Liberty Hill Inn, on the corner of Willow Street and Route 6A, a leg was found in the wall during a major renovation project.

Years later, this still remains an unsolved case. The rightful owner has never attempted to claim his missing leg and no stories or records exist about either a missing person or a person who "lost a leg" during the period the house was under construction. There are some who say the leg may have belonged to one of those involved in rumrunning.

Yarmouth was a hotbed for illegal liquor being smuggled ashore during these notorious years, both on the bay side at Wharf Lane and Bass Hole, and on the south coast at a place appropriately named today, "Smugglers Beach."

Who knows…some day the spirit may reveal himself.

134 OLD KING'S HIGHWAY

Captain Howes's Cottage
Sad Times

This ornate gingerbread Gothic was built as a summer "cottage" for Captain Frederick Howes and his family. Captain Howes is best known for his invention of the Howes rig, a double sail that operated far more efficiently and with less manpower than a single sail. The Howes rig allowed shipowners to reduce the number of crewmen as well as gain speed from the sails. When Howes built his home around 1850, it might well have been created as a way for him and his wife to get over a tragedy that occurred a few years earlier. Captain Howes's wife was the former Eliza Meriam.

Late in 1845, Eliza's sister, twenty-eight-year-old Mary Meriam, paid the family a visit. She later died of scarlet fever on November 17 of the same year. It is believed that she may have passed this dreaded disease on to the Howes family. At least two of the Howes's children contracted the disease, with two-year-old Lucy dying on December 27 and her four-year-old brother Frederick dying four days later.

During the terrible gale of December 30, 1853, the "cottage" suffered severe damage—all the chimneys were blown down. The house wasn't the panacea that Howes hoped it would be, and in 1857, he offered the house for sale. Due to the bad financial times, he was unable to sell the property. When Howes died in 1882, his funeral was held at the cottage.

In the more recent past, the house had been converted to a restaurant (now the Optimist Café). Employees have their own stories about ghosts in the building, ranging from hearing footsteps when first entering to finding lights on that had been shut off. On one occasion, a voice came through the speaker of the radio, even though the radio was turned off. Employees believe this to be Emily, a daughter of Frederick Howes. Perhaps over the years the name of the ghost has been changed slightly, as Howes had a daughter name Eliza. She would have been ten years old at the time of the sale in 1857.

Paranormal investigators have visited the building and have found much activity. One vision was of people in shackles, leading the investigators to wonder if this house was part of the underground railroad, which brought fugitive slaves north in the years before the Civil War. Why these fugitives would still be in shackles wasn't explained. The house has a varied and interesting past and is a place of interest to those who believe in the supernatural.

A Cape Cod Bed-and-Breakfast
New Friends

We wanted to vacation on Cape Cod, but we wanted it to be a bit more personal than just going to the beach and staying in a motel. We have two children, ages nine and eleven, and we decided to bring them with us—a family vacation. Our choice for lodging for the two nights was a local bed-

and-breakfast. We hoped they wouldn't be bored. The first night, we put them to bed and stayed downstairs talking to the innkeeper. We heard the kids talking and laughing softly. When we went to bed, there were still noises.

The next morning, after breakfast, we went to the beach. I asked the children if they were having a good time. "Last night was a blast," my younger son said. "We met two kids who lived at the inn and we talked and played almost all night. They knew plenty of games that didn't need computers and we really had fun!"

When we arrived back at the bed-and-breakfast that evening, we talked with the innkeeper about the children. "Children?" replied the owner. "There haven't been kids here in more than seventy-five years. The previous owners had two children who tragically died in a storm, and no one who has owned this inn since has had children."

I didn't ask any other questions, and the next day we packed up and left. Our children played their newfound games in the car on the way home, while my husband and I shook our heads in amazement.

Myths and Legends
of the Sea

The stories in this chapter are a combination of myths and recorded history—sometimes interwoven. Although we cannot vouch for the actual sightings, we believe the recorded information was accurate at the time it was written.

Up to now, enchanted whales have not been mentioned. But Cape lore is full of them. They range from Ichabod Paddock's encounter with a whale named Crook Jaw, to the finback known as Long John who took a mermaid for a ride in Cape Cod Bay. And then there is Goodie Hallet, who supposedly lived inside a whale known as the "Whistling Whale." Their stories follow.

Ichabod Paddock Legends

Ichabod Paddock legends come from a variety of sources. The authors have written this legend to coincide with the actual time Ichabod lived—the 1700s.

Mermaids and sea serpents, in the design of Edward Gorey, were painted on a whale by three Rhode Island School of Design students. This whale may be seen in the Edward Gorey house. *Photo courtesy of the Edward Gorey house.*

The Mermaid

Ichabod Paddock met a mermaid as a result of a run-in with a whale by the name of Crook Jaw. Crook Jaw couldn't be harpooned. None of the harpoons Ichabod tossed penetrated the whale's skin.

Ichabod wouldn't give up. The next time he met up with Crook Jaw, Ichabod dove into the ocean. With his knife between his teeth, he swam to the whale and waited for him to open his jaws. The whale yawned, and in swam Ichabod.

Ichabod was surprised by what he found inside. There was a door of a ship's cabin straight ahead of him. Opening the door he found two beings playing cards. One was a beautiful green-eyed mermaid, with blond hair; the other was the devil. As Ichabod watched, the devil threw down his cards and swore. He glared at Ichabod and then vanished.

Ichabod apologized to the mermaid for interrupting and then asked what the stakes were. The mermaid laughed and said, "Stakes, Captain Paddock? You were the stakes!"

Meanwhile, back on Ichabod's whaleboat, his crew all but gave him up for lost. But being a loyal crew, they waited out the night beside the unmoving Crook Jaw. The next morning, asleep at their oars, the crew was awakened by the sound of Ichabod swimming toward them.

Ichabod and his crew went whaling that evening. Once again, he spent the night in the stomach of the whale. This continued for several nights until Ichabod's wife, hearing some of the rumors told by the crew, grew suspicious.

The next time Ichabod came ashore, his wife—a pretty woman less than thirty years of age—gave him a gift: a shiny, newly forged harpoon. When Ichabod wanted to go whaling the next day, his wife asked him to take her father along. Soon Crook Jaw was found.

Ichabod knew it would be impossible to harpoon the whale. He watched as his father-in-law took the new harpoon and threw it, striking the whale. Surprisingly, the harpoon held, and Crook Jaw was soon being towed back to land. When they cut into the whale, Ichabod found more surprises. Where there had once been a ship's cabin, all he found was yellow seaweed and two green shells.

After Ichabod and his family left Nantucket and returned to Yarmouth, his wife confessed to what she had done. It was not an iron harpoon she had given him; instead, it had been made of silver—the only metal that will pierce the heart of a witch.

Captain Ichabod Paddock—Whaler of Nantucket

Anne Malcolmson's *Captain Ichabod Paddock—Whaler of Nantucket* (Walker and Co, 1970) sets the date of Ichabod's exploits much later, probably in the 1800s. It is a children's story about a whaler who goes on a ten-year cruise. The mermaid is a redhead, with bright green scales. The card game being played is rummy and the mermaid served Ichabod supper every Tuesday.

The men on his vessel knew Ichabod was bewitched. The whale, Crook Jaw, was led by the devil, and eventually they ended up in Nantucket Harbor. Mrs. Paddock also knew Ichabod was bewitched when she saw him jump overboard and swim to the whale.

She melted down all her silver and made a small silver harpoon, just big enough for her hand. She was the harpooner who killed Crook Jaw. In the stomach, they found a piece of green seaweed in the shape of a mermaid. Where the hair would have been, the seaweed was bright red.

Crook Jaw

Caron Lee Cohen's book, *Crook Jaw* (Henry Holt and Company, 1997), takes much more liberty with Paddock's actual past. He is credited with killing 431 whales by the age of ten while aboard his boat, *Blubber Boiler*. His wife's name is Smilinda. As with the other tales, Ichabod falls under the spell of a witch, this one wearing red shoes. The final result is the same as in the other tales.

The Narrow Land

Elizabeth Reynard's book, *The Narrow Land* (Houghton Mifflin, 1962), discusses folk chronicles of old Cape Cod. Reynard writes of Ichabod Paddock, the "whale master," before he traveled to Nantucket to teach whaling.

Ichabod was in Truro at the time. He was waiting for money from England when a "merwoman", a sea witch, asked him to kill a finback whale named Long John. The mermaid/witch was angry because Long John wouldn't give her a ride on his back. The Seed-Corners Company, a Truro whaling company, had long been unable to kill Long John.

In her anger, the mermaid offered a string of pearls to the person who killed the whale. Ichabod was offered not only the pearls, but also love and gold. He refused, and instead told her to relay to the whale that he would never hunt him if the whale took the mermaid on his head for a ride around the Cape.

The mermaid hurried to Lost Island, home of Long John, where Long John agreed. She fashioned a bridle out of weeds and they began their voyage around the Cape. When the finback reached Sandwich, he "spouted high," and the mermaid was blown high into the sky. She landed in Sandwich Pond and has lived there ever since.

The Seed-Corners Company, a whaling company, actually existed about forty years after Ichabod Paddock had died.

A Paddock's Road sign. In Dennis, Paddock's Road runs through the area where the Paddocks lived. In the seventeenth and eighteenth centuries, this area was part of Yarmouth.

Maria "Goodie" Hallet

Yarmouth lore places the infamous Goodie Hallet as a barmaid at the Old Yarmouth Inn shortly after it opened, but it was her exploits on the lower Cape that made her famous. Truro believed she was the wife of a minister from Eastham. Eastham maintained that she was the "furrin" wife of a Truro sea captain. Others said that she lived in a hut in the midst of dunes reputed to be on the town line between Eastham and Wellfleet. Some believed she was

Native American; others said she was white and used a cat and a gray goat in her spells. The goat was reputed to have had a glass eye. Others said she was run out of Eastham and came to Yarmouth, where she became a tavern maid at the Old Yarmouth Inn.

There are many stories about Goodie Hallet. Some seem to blend her exploits with those of Delia Roach of Wellfleet, or those of a witch who wore red shoes from Truro. She

The sign of the Old Yarmouth Inn. As the sign states, the inn was opened in the seventeenth century, at the time Goodie Hallet was living.

could have been any of these, or perhaps she was just the unfortunate girlfriend of a pirate.

The Pirate Lore

Goodie was born in 1700. As a young teenager, she was seduced by the pirate Sam Bellamy. The following winter, she was apprehended in a barn with her dead baby. After being arrested, she was given a whipping at the town's whipping post and was thrown into the Eastham jail to await trial for murder. While there, a stranger walked by and saw her. He was dressed in fine French clothes. His gaze kept her spellbound. The stranger took one of the iron bars in the window and flicked it away. He offered to free her if she would sign a paper. Being illiterate, she signed with an X and escaped from the jail. Was this the devil? Did Goodie make a pact with him?

The Sea Witch of Billingsgate

Some say Goodie was the famous sea witch of Billingsgate with a number of exploits to her credit. After being stoned as a witch, Goodie went to Billingsgate Island (Wellfleet) and lived in a small hut alone. Her main effort seemed to have been to capture the souls of dead seamen. Her friends, a black cat and a black goat, were said to ride on the backs of porpoises, following in the wake of ships. Seamen setting out for the Grand Banks would exclaim, whenever they saw two green eyes staring from the spume, "That be Goodie Hallet's friends waitin' to pick up souls. Reef sail, a squall's to windward." A few moments later, low in the sky would hang a cloud as black and portentous as the witch's cat's tail.

Goodie could hold a ship in port by putting her cat under a "berry-bushel." A dead calm or contrary wind was the result. "The Old Woman has got the cat under the half bushel" was a proverb used among the seagoing men when contrary winds blew.

Some say she lost this ability when Portuguese sailors found an effective antidote—take the heart of a dead calf, stick it with pins and drop it down a chimney. The last known appearance of this sea witch was about 1800.

Who Is the Witch with the Red Shoes?

At times, writers have confused Goodie's pranks with those of the red-shoed witch of Truro, whose broomstick put out the seamen's light that burned in the old meetinghouse on the Hill of Storms. Six vessels were wrecked in the darkness, twenty lives were lost and Goodie, who was known to hate sailors, was accused of the crime.

Around the same time, a Native American woman from Wellfleet, Delia Roach, heard that people had accused her of being the witch. She marched herself down to the town clerk's office, wanting to get it straightened out—she was not a witch! But the clerk noticed a brief spot of scarlet beneath the hem of her skirt, first on the right, then on the left. The red shoes? The town believed the clerk's story of the red shoes, and in 1802, it voted to repair her house and make her comfortable—just to keep her from doing anything to them! If this was Goodie, she would have been 102 years old.

More Folklore

It was also said that Goodie took up residence in a whale. They would cruise about with a ship's light hung on the whale's tail. She lured ships onto sandbars, took men off of them at night and rode them like a horse up and down the beaches of Cape Cod, returning them in the morning, exhausted from their "work." She was believed to have dabbled with the weather, sometimes creating hurricanes.

Author Elizabeth Reynard puts a different twist on Goodie Hallet. In her version, Goodie Hallet lived within a whale for more than a century. Through the courtesy of Lucifer, she possessed the body of a whale known as the Whistlin' Whale. She and the devil played many games of "saltwater dice," with Goodie repeatedly defeating him. One night, he became exceedingly upset and choked her to death. He then left the Whistlin' Whale. Many years later, the Seed-Corners Company of Truro killed the whale. They reported to have found a pair of red lacquer shoes in its belly.

Who Was Goodie Hallet?

You have to wonder where Goodie found time to be a tavern maid at the Old Yarmouth Inn. Still, Yarmouth claims her and glorifies the fact that it was only in Yarmouth that she did not try to pull any magical tricks on sailors or landsmen. But then, people spending an evening at the tavern might have heard a shriek mingling with the high sea wind. They would draw their cloaks about them and murmur, "That be poor Goodie, dancin' with the lost souls." Postriders on King's Highway spurred their mounts after dusk and didn't risk an unaware glance into the hollow. Even the horses sensed danger, for they pushed on with a burst of speed.

SEA MONSTERS AND STRANGE CREATURES AROUND CAPE COD

The waters surrounding Cape Cod have had more recorded sightings of strange sea creatures than almost anywhere else on earth. Massachusetts Bay, Cape Cod Bay and the waters south of the Cape seem to teem with these creatures if one is to believe all of the sightings.

Recorded Sightings
Cape Cod—August 4, 1609

Explorer Henry Hudson's crew, while stopped at Cape Cod on August 4, 1609, recorded what is believed to be the first written contact with a mermaid. They had a previous encounter with a mermaid near Russia in June 1608. One might suspect that either the grog they were drinking or their imaginations caused these sightings, as they are one of the few crews to have had more than one experience with sea creatures. Perhaps the wild grapes that Hudson's crew found had fermented.

1639

The first recorded encounter by colonists occurred in 1639. Massachusetts colonists wrote of a sea serpent playing in the waters of Nahant Bay. They were digging clams at the time of the sighting. Native Americans in the area also had tales of a sea serpent they had seen in earlier times. John Josselyn separately recorded a conversation with English seamen who had seen the monster the same year sunning itself on the rocks off Cape Ann.

Boston—September 28, 1719

Eighty years later, the following appeared in the *Boston Gazette*.

On the 17 Instant there appears in Cape-Cod harbour [Cape Cod was the name by which Provincetown was known until it became a separate town in 1729] *a strange creature, his head like a Lyons, with very large Teeth, Ears hanging down, a large Beard, a long Beard with curling hair on his head, his Body about 16 foot long, a round buttock, with a short Tayle of a yellowish colour, the Whale boats gave him chase, he was very fierce and gnashed his teeth with great rage when they attackt him, he was shot at 3 times and Wounded, when he rose out of the Water he always faced the boats in that angry manner, the Harpaniers struck at him, but in vaine, for after 5 hours chase, he took him to sea again. None of the people ever saw his like before.*

"The Provincetown Sea Monster" was written in 1719, shortly after the *Boston Gazette* was founded. James Franklin,

A sea monster from an eighteenth-century map of America. The monster looks very similar to those later reported around Cape Cod.

printer of the *Gazette*, was Benjamin Franklin's older brother. John Miller and Tim Smith, editors of *Cape Cod Stories* (Chronicle Books, 1996), attributed this article to Benjamin Franklin, the uncle of the famous Patriot and inventor. It is more likely to have been by the Patriot himself. He had written articles for his brother in the past, especially while James was editor of the *New England Courant*.

Incredibly, the description of the sea monster closely resembled the drawing of a creature shown on a 1638 Dutch map of the area. It was unlikely that the Franklins would have seen the map.

Gloucester—August 1817

Sightings became more common in the nineteenth century. In August 1817, Gloucester had one of the more famous incidents. During that month, the monster played in Gloucester Harbor and Massachusetts Bay, where more than two hundred witnesses saw it. It was generally described as a snakelike serpent, between fifty and ninety feet long, with a head the size of a horse and the body about three feet in diameter. One report from a ship's carpenter named Matthew Gaffney mentioned that the serpent swam vertically through the water, like a caterpillar.

1818

The following year, not too far from Stellwagen Bank, a packet boat bound for Maine from Boston saw a sea monster. Captain Shubael West and fifteen others saw a sea serpent engaged in a fight with a humpback whale.

> *The serpent threw up his tail from 25–30 feet in a perpendicular direction, striking the whale with it. At the same time, he raised his head 15 or 20 feet in the air, as if taking a view of the surface of the sea. After being seen in this position a few minutes, the serpent disappeared.*

1830–1859

Sightings of sea serpents were common during this period of time. In the 1830s, off the coast of Long Island, the schooner *Sally* reportedly had a fight with a sea serpent. In 1833, a sea monster became such a nuisance that whaling crews were sent out from around Massachusetts Bay to get rid of it. There is no record of them catching the creature. In 1859, the *British Banner* reported another attack on a sailing vessel, where the description of the monster matched the Gloucester sightings, although it now had a horn on its head. An English warship also noted that it saw a sea monster swim by, but without incident or attack.

After the Civil War, the famous showman P.T. Barnum offered a reward of $1,000 to anyone who would bring him one, dead or alive. He did this because fishermen had been hesitant to bring the creature in, fearing it would spoil their catch. No one took him up on his offer.

Provincetown—1886

In 1886, the Provincetown town crier, George Washington Ready, shocked the Cape by bringing an article to the *Yarmouth Register* about sighting a sea serpent. This one was seen in Provincetown. It was at Herring Cove where Mr. Ready first saw the sea monster. It was spouting water to heights of fifty feet or more. He hid behind some bushes as the monster passed close to shore.

In the *Yarmouth Register* of 1886, Ready reported:

> *It had a slow, undulating motion as it wagged its head, as big as a 200 gallon cask. It was about 300 feet long and about 12 feet in diameter. The body was covered with scales as large as the head of a fish barrel, and were colored alternately green, red, and blue. The open mouth disclosed four rows of teeth, which glistened like polished ivory, and were at least two feet long, while on the extreme end of the head or nose, extended a tusk or horn at least eight feet in length. The creature had six eyes as large as good sized dinner plates and they were*

*placed at the end of moveable projections. With these, the
creature could see ahead, behind, and sideways*

Ready also stated the creature smelled of sulfur. He thought
people might doubt him, so he included his affidavit:

*I, George Washington Ready, do testify that the foregoing
statement is correct. It is a true description of the serpent
as he appeared to me on that morning, and I was not
unduly excited by liquor or otherwise. George W. Ready.*

During the nineteenth century, there were nearly two
hundred different sightings recorded.

Gulf of Maine—1912

The twentieth century had its share of sightings. In 1912, the
Philomena, a mackerel fishing boat, caught a sea monster in its
nets off the Gulf of Maine. Two other fishing vessels came
to help in the two-hour battle. They decided to cut loose the
eighty-foot monster, rather than drag it in, as they thought it
would endanger the vessel's safety.

Orleans—January 17, 1936

Orleans had its own sea monster. During the Depression, the
following article appeared:

Orleans, Jan 17, 1936—Somewhere in the briny deep that wash the Nauset strand, Orleans Coast Guards swear sea serpents with tongues shaped like fish tails, swivel jointed necks and 200 teeth mounted in cavernous jaws stalk their prey. Surf man Fred Moll found the remains of such a critter on the beach below the station yesterday. All that remains of the marine mystery is a grinning head with a few inches of what appears to be a snake-like body attached.

For a week, the whole of Cape Cod was alive with rumors. Even though it was winter, the story didn't keep anyone out of the water. A week later, three men spoiled the suspense. Everett Eldredge Jr., Ed Taylor and John Nickerson identified the skull as belonging to a dolphin. So much for that sea serpent!

The Biggest Story Yet

No article on sea monsters would be complete without mentioning author Scott Corbett's sea captain. The captain saw some of the strangest sea creatures. One day, in the early 1900s, he took a party out sailing. Onboard was a typical brash summer visitor, a young fellow who knew more and had always seen bigger and better things than anyone else. This young man asked the captain what was the largest fish he had ever seen.

"Well, I don't rightly know what 'twas," said the captain, "but it was monstrously big, and had a tremendous mouth, and it blew water up in the air now and then."

"Why that was a whale," the young man snickered scornfully, but the captain shook his head.

"No, no—we was baiting with whales."

As for "new" sightings, we're not sure, as our research was confined to the period leading up to the twentieth century. But we all know history repeats itself. The next time you're at the beach or sailing the bays, remember to keep an eye on the water. You never know what you might see.

MIDSUMMER'S EVE
The Myth of Midsummer's Eve

It is believed that on the evening of the June 23, ghost ships rise from their watery graves to continue their journeys. Why the twenty-third? The day has been known by a variety of names throughout history. The names, in fact, may provide clues as to why this is such a ghostly night. It has been called Midsummer's Eve, Johnsmas, Jack's Night, St. John the Baptist's birthday and Sailorman's Eve. Astrologically, on this date, the sun enters the water sign of Cancer, making water a natural part of the celebration. For centuries, oceans have had an aura of being magical. June 23 was chosen to

Two characters in the Midsummer's Eve program put on by the Historical Society of Old Yarmouth at Bass Hole in 2006. *Photo courtesy of Ted Weissberger.*

celebrate the birthday of John the Baptist, and the date ties in with the pagan rituals for the summer solstice. The Celts chose June 24 as the date for their solstice celebration. Since their day ran from sundown to sundown, the evening of June 23 fell within it.

In past centuries, Cape Cod and other maritime areas have found this date to be one of the more ghostly times of the year. Some places, including Austria and South America, still celebrate this evening. Local lore and myths stated that on the night of the twenty-third, the ghosts show themselves. Interestingly, the ghosts were not of people, but of vessels that had been lost at sea.

In Austria and South America, the evening is celebrated with candle boats, or little boats set on fire and floated on bodies of water. Fire is associated with this water celebration, and in some parts of the world bonfires are lit to ward off the evil spirits. People jump over the bonfires for good luck. Bad luck comes instantly if you miss the jump!

Cape Cod

Early colonists to America brought these beliefs and fears with them. Mythology turned to custom, and in the eighteenth and nineteenth centuries, Cape Codders believed that vessels that met untimely endings would reappear on this evening.

An incredible number of vessels were wrecked on or near Cape Cod. There were over 500 recorded shipwrecks in the mid-nineteenth century. Between 1880 and 1903, an additional 540 vessels ended up wrecked ashore. Since both fire and water were included in the myths of Midsummer's Eve, vessels that burned and sank were especially likely to reappear. Cape Codders had plenty of subjects for this very ghostly occurrence.

The Bark Burlington

Late in 1840, the bark *Burlington* caught fire and sank in the Atlantic. Captained by Bangs Hallet of Yarmouth Port, the *Burlington* was carrying cotton to Europe when it was hit by lightning, which traveled down the mast and set fire to the cargo. Hallet and his crew covered opened areas of the deck with canvas in an attempt to suffocate the fire. Afterward, they drilled holes in the deck at places that were warm and pumped seawater into them to douse the flames.

Conditions worsened as a "complete" hurricane roared through the *Burlington*'s location, requiring the crew to ride out the storm tied to the deck and masts of the burning ship. When the storm subsided, the captain declared the ship unsalvageable, and he and the crew boarded longboats and abandoned ship. Their luck changed when a British ship, the *St. James*, came on the scene and all were rescued.

Accounts of the disaster were reported in the *Yarmouth Register*. The story was based on the recollections of the *Burlington*'s crew. Since then, on Midsummer's Eve, some have noticed a glow on the horizon and believe it to be the *Burlington*, trying to return to Bangs Hallet's home port of Yarmouth.

The Pirate Ship Widah

The *Widah*, a pirate ship belonging to Sam Bellamy, was wrecked off the coast of Truro in 1717. Prior to the wreck, there had been stories of Bellamy enticing a fifteen-year-old girl from Eastham, Maria "Goodie" Hallet, into a relationship that resulted in the birth of an illegitimate child. Afterward, tales of Goodie being a witch spread through the town. Some of the townspeople believed the *Widah* was bewitched by Goodie and that she caused it to wreck. Only two crewmen survived. Bellamy was not one of them.

It's said that on Midsummer's Eve, the *Widah* again sets sail, the pirate Bellamy in command, in an attempt to round the tip of Cape Cod and complete the journey that previously ended in disaster.

The remains of the *Widah* were salvaged and today can be seen in Provincetown.

The Fishing Fleet

Each town has its own vessels that locals look for on this strange night. No town has a sadder search than Truro, as its inhabitants look to the north in hopes of seeing their fishing schooners return. In October 1841, a monstrous gale hit the fleet of fishing vessels off Georges Bank. A total of eighty-four souls were lost during the gale: fifty-seven men from Truro, twenty from Dennis and seven from Yarmouth. While two Truro crews managed to make it home safely, only one fishing schooner returned. Its name—the *Water Witch.* One Truro schooner, the *Pomona*, drifted bottom up into Wellfleet Harbor, three of its crew found dead in the cabin.

Oddly, the only schooner no one searches for on Midsummer's Eve is the one named for a witch.

The Steamer Pacific

Not all of the vessels seen are powered by sail. The *Pacific*, a transatlantic steamer built for Edward Knight Collins of Truro, first sailed for Europe in 1849. It was so fast that some have said it won a trophy from England for the fastest crossing of the Atlantic. Collins liked captains who worked their vessels for every ounce of speed. He hired Captain Asa Eldridge after Eldridge had taken the clipper ship *Red Jacket* from New York to Liverpool in a record time of thirteen days and one hour.

Eldridge felt the pressure to keep up with speed crossings. In January 1856, the *Pacific* left Liverpool bound for New York. It was Captain Eldridge's first voyage on the steamer. The *Pacific* never made port. Its disappearance was a cause for much speculation. The papers of the time felt that it must have hit an iceberg in the North Atlantic, taking 45 passengers and the crew of 141 to their icy deaths.

In 1986, the true location of the steamer was found when a fishing vessel in the Irish Sea snagged its nets somewhere between Angle Sea and the Isle of Man. The cause of the snag was later determined to be the wreck of the *Pacific*. Conjecture now suggests that the steamer experienced a boiler explosion, causing the vessel to sink immediately with no survivors. On Midsummer's Eve, the *Pacific* is rumored to rise from its watery grave to finish its speed crossing.

The HMS Somerset

Not all of the ghost vessels seen on Midsummer's Eve are American. One frequently mentioned is the HMS *Somerset*, a sixty-four-gun British man-of-war, made famous by Longfellow's poem about Paul Revere. During the American Revolution, the *Somerset* patrolled the waters off Cape Cod. Provincetown, nearly deserted during this period, was common anchorage for British warships. On a stormy night in 1778, the *Somerset* ran aground on the sandbar near Dead Man's Hollow, not far from the Highlands in North Truro. The crew of 480 soldiers and sailors were "rescued" by Americans and were marched to Boston as prisoners of war.

The bones of the *Somerset* have appeared on occasion, especially after severe storms or spring tides. On Midsummer's Eve, the *Somerset* is said to rise and bring terror to the entire Cape population as it continues its deadly mission to subdue colonial malcontents.

The Race Is On

Not all vessels viewed on Midsummer's Eve had disastrous endings. Most well known are the packets of the towns

A sketch of the packet *Mail*, one of several that plied their trades between Yarmouth Port and Boston. *Courtesy of Haynes Mahoney, author of* Yarmouth's Proud Packets.

bordering Cape Cod Bay. The packets, freight- and passenger-carrying sloops and schooners were put out of business by the arrival of the railroads in the 1850s. On the night of June 23, one can watch the return of the packets, racing from their home ports to Boston. The races between the packets of Yarmouth and Barnstable were legendary; often reported in local papers, they were a source of immense pride. Many a wager was placed on the outcome.

Today, the skeleton of an unknown schooner, perhaps a packet from Yarmouth, lies on a sandbar near the channel that leads to Yarmouth's Central Wharf, not far from Sandy Neck lighthouse. Could this be one of the vessels that appear on Midsummer's Eve?

Prairie Schooners

Elizabeth Reynard, author of *The Narrow Land*, tied other sightings to this maritime night. She included wagons built in the 1840s and '50s by the Keith Car Works of Sandwich. In her book, she related that wagons were "seen" on the evening of June 23 traveling east. Why did these wagons try to get back to Sandwich? They were prairie schooners— those hardy wagons used by settlers heading west. Reynard speculated that the "schooners" were returning to where they were built.

Viewing Locations

Where are the best places to view these ghostly vessels? No town can claim exclusive rights to sightings. Many of the vessels are attempting to get to port. The ports with the most sightings are Provincetown, Wellfleet, Corporation Beach in Dennis, the mouth of Bass River and Lewis Bay. In addition, places with boardwalks, such as Yarmouth and Sandwich, are especially good viewing locations. Falmouth also has a number of great viewing spots. What should you bring? Binoculars, an open mind and a good imagination. Children usually spot far more vessels than adults!

FISHERMEN SUPERSTITIONS

Sailors are said to be very superstitious. Below are several "sayings" from the eighteenth and nineteenth centuries. Most determined the amount and/or type of luck you would have if you obeyed the superstition. For those who either didn't believe or disobeyed, there was always the evening of June 23 to change their "luck."

1) Many sailors believe a woman onboard is bad luck. The origin of the myth related to fact that women were a distraction to men and accidents happened when men were distracted from what they were doing. However, a woman with her breasts bared is known to calm seas, which is

why many sailing vessels of this period were adorned with figureheads of this motif.

2) Don't sail on Fridays. It is an unlucky day. Sunday is the best day (but not during Puritan times) and it led to the old adage—Sunday sail, never fail.

3) Good days and bad days to sail were tied closely to the Bible. Christ was crucified on Friday—bad day. He was resurrected on Sunday—good day. On the first Monday in April, Cain slew Abel—bad day. Second Monday in August, Sodom and Gomorrah were destroyed—bad day to sail.

Regarding the vessel itself:

1) Place a silver coin under the masthead for good luck.

2) A stolen piece of wood, made into part of the keel, will make the ship faster.

3) It is bad luck to step onto a vessel with your left foot first.

4) Pour wine on the deck as a good luck offering.

5) Don't stick a knife in a wooden mast.

6) Coil all line on a vessel clockwise.

7) Throw back the first fish you catch and you'll be lucky all day.

8) If you count the number of fish you caught, you won't catch any more that day.

9) It is bad luck to say the word "pig" while fishing.

10) If you dream of fish, someone you know is pregnant. Wives especially didn't want fishermen dreaming of work!
11) Don't use a knife with a white handle. These knives are tools of witches and considered unlucky.

WOMEN

Women with mystical powers have occupied a major place in the lore and history of Cape Cod. Some are reputed to be witches; others have the power to heal. All were real persons, although their stories may lead you to wonder. In this chapter, we will recount several stories from the mid-Cape area.

DEB OF DEB'S HILL

Written by Mary Bray in 1915 for the *Cape Cod Magazine*, Deb's story tells of a mysterious woman who lived in a small cabin upon a hill within the town of Yarmouth. Deb's Hill, more commonly known as German Hill, lies just north of Route 6. Great Western Road runs up and over the hill. The legend of Deb's Hill is copied exactly as Mary Bray wrote it:

Deb was by no means a myth—scarcely a tradition. She was a very real personage. Her doings and sayings are, however, somewhat traditional, since they have come orally to this generation from a preceding one. At some period in her life, Deb had, doubtless, a surname, but if so, it had dropped away from her in the obscurity of the past. In this, however, she was scarcely worse off than some royal personages that one hears of, though they to be sure make up for the latter deficiency by a super fluidity of individual names, while Deb was known only by this three-letter contraction.

Deb was tall and muscular, a woman of the Meg Merrill type. She had not, perhaps, quite so much the air of a prophetess, judging from the reports that still linger in the vicinity of her haunts, but we cannot say what she might have been made to appear, under the transforming imagination of Scott.

She had, or pretended to have, similar gifts. If you crossed her palm with a bit of silver, she would trace wonderful fortunes on your own. She shuffled cards with a mysterious air—though some occult force controlled the combinations and she gazed at the floating tea leaves in the bottom of a cup with the eye of a seeress.

She lived in a small house of two rooms, situated on a pine-crowned hill, about two miles from the village. The smallness of the hut seemed to accentuate her size. Her head reached nearly to the un-ceiled roof; her presence appeared to pervade the whole building.

The front room, into which one entered directly from the outside, was her living room. It had two small windows and a fireplace. There she, presumably, cooked, ate, and slept. Back of it was another small room, scarcely larger than a closet. About this hung an air of mystery. She seldom allowed anyone but herself to enter it, yet she made frequent trips into it and back again for no apparent purpose. She could have used it for a storeroom, if she ever had any stores to put in it, which is doubtful. Or, it may have been connected in some way with her spells and divinations.

Deb's nationality was a problem. That she had some Indian blood in her veins was certain. There were unmistakable evidences of this in her tall straight figure, her deep-set eyes and the copper-colored tint of her skin. Tradition said that she was also of gypsy origin, because she was given to long periods of wandering. She would now and then be missing for days—even weeks. She gave no hint of her going, or of her destination or object. She simply put two nails over her door during such times of her absence. And such was her awesome reputation that these were never withdrawn, nor her hut invaded, even by mischievous boys.

During the warm weather, Deb often came to the village with bunches of herbs and buckets of blueberries, beach plums, and wild grapes in their respective seasons. These she would sell at various prices, according to her mood of the moment. In the winter, she lived chiefly upon divination and charity.

So homogeneous was the population of the Cape in those days that before leaving their homes, people seldom locked their doors. It would happen now and then that a housekeeper, coming back from an entertainment or a friendly visit with a neighbor, would find that her pantry had been invaded during her absence.

If she found ginger and flour scattered about and her molasses jug, milk pitcher and yeast lacking part of their content, she would at once surmise that Deb had been

Deb's Hill sign. Located on Great Western Road in Yarmouth, where it travels over German Hill, is the Deb's Hill condominium complex. In the nineteenth century, German Hill was known as Deb's Hill by the locals.

there, and had been making bread or gingerbread to take home with her.

People were neighborly in those days, and nobody protested against this habit. Deb was never known to take anything else that did not belong to her. She would have scorned to steal! But to make for herself needed food in a convenient household, she regarded as a right.

Deb long ago disappeared from the haunts of men. When, where or how her exit from earth took place, neither her history nor tradition has said. Her hut is no longer, but the hill remains, bearing the crown of pines of yore. Today, some still referred to the area as Deb's Hill.

SOPHIE ANN KELLEY CHASE

Approximately 150 years later, an entirely different kind of witch lived on the north side of Yarmouth. Her name was Aunt Sophie Ann Kelley Chase. She supposedly had magical powers, being the seventh daughter of a seventh son. Lore has long held that the seventh son of a seventh son will be a werewolf. Could this mean that the seventh daughter of the seventh son has magical powers? The lore is not clear when it comes to women. Aunt Sophie, born in 1830, never had children. In her later life, she lived alone in an old house. The reclusiveness probably made her seem strange to the people

The Hockanom "witch" house, located near Route 6A in Yarmouth. The house (no longer there) was located just west of the entrance to King's Way on the north side of the road.

of her time. She died in her eighties, in the years just before World War I.

The Witch of Hockanom

Many in Yarmouth called Aunt Sophie a witch. Willie and George Bray, brothers, were two farmers who lived fairly close to her on Bray Farm and they were two of her biggest defenders. While they agreed that she seemed to have magical powers, she only used them to help people and therefore should not be called a witch.

The "witch's" house is no longer there, having been torn down a number of years ago. It was located east of Hockanom Road on the north side of Old King's Highway.

The house had a hip roof and two stories, making it quite distinctive. It was the original homestead of Gorham Bray.

Aunt Sophie's Visions

When she first went to school as a child, Sophie seemed to know each lesson before it was presented without prior knowledge of the lesson or studying. She left school at an early age, probably at the teacher's urging.

Throughout her life, she knew of things without being told of them. Sea captains would quiz her about faraway ports. Aunt Sophie had never left Yarmouth, but she would close her eyes, sit back in her rocker and in a few minutes open them again. She would tell the captains about the faraway areas, with specifics about the port city, as well as the weather. The captains related that she was totally accurate, giving details that only a person who had visited these places would have known.

Mystical Powers

Aunt Sophie had the power to heal people. People came from all over the Cape to see her. While most of these incidents aren't recorded, there is one involving a crippled woman who had been bedridden for a number of years. When her husband brought her to see Aunt Sophie, Sophie told the woman to get up and move around. The woman was able to get up and walk. She left Aunt Sophie's house under her own power.

Of course there were doubters. Author Katharine Crosby related that the village bully, name unknown, boasted that Aunt Sophie couldn't do anything to him. He went to her house and started to talk "rough." She merely touched him, and he landed on the floor, unable to move. The bully quickly realized he had met his match and wanted to leave, but Aunt Sophie left him there on the floor for some time before he was allowed to go. He never bothered her again.

Sadly, few of her other good works were recorded. All we have are apocryphal (mythical) anecdotes. However, it is certain that there was something mystical and magical about this fine lady.

MARY DUNN

A Life of Fact and Fiction

Mary Dunn was an extraordinary woman by all accounts. In 1976, the late Margaret Milliken wrote the following poem about Mary.

What has Mary Dunn Done?
What has Mary Dunn done
What did Mary Dunn do

That brought her fame?
Her good home brew

And her open door
To any who came
By the Pond, By the Road,
That keeps her name.

The Myths of Mary Dunn

Mary Dunn may have more false stories written about her than any other woman on Cape Cod. Charles Swift, the editor of the *Yarmouth Register* and author of the *History of Yarmouth*, is responsible for creating the myths of Mary Dunn being a witch, prophet and fortuneteller. Swift referred to Mary Dunn as a Native American, and gave her magical powers. Supposedly, she was accused of using her witchery to wreck a Swedish vessel off Sandy Neck. In his article, written in 1896, he asserted that Mary was more than a hundred years old.

The myths about Mary are many, and they have grown over the years. They include:

1) Mary Dunn was a fugitive slave who escaped from the South onboard a Cape Cod schooner.
2) Mary Dunn's husband was a former slave who favored the South and recruited soldiers on Cape Cod for the Confederacy.

Mary Dunn Road. The road on which Mary Dunn lived connects Route 6A with Hyannis. Mary Dunn lived about a mile from this sign.

3) Mary Dunn was a full-blooded Native American.
4) Mary Dunn was a witch.
5) Mary Dunn died with a snake twisted around her neck, and her body disappeared.

The Family of Mary Dunn

Mary Dunn was a Cape Cod native, not an escaped slave, despite the claims of five writers, including Donald Trayser,

Margaret Milliken, Betty Burkes, Eugene Green and William Sachse. According to the Yarmouth town records, Mary was born on July 6, 1778, the daughter of Boston Boston and Lucy.

Boston Boston was listed as a "Negro," one of five slaves Ebenezer Hinckley of Barnstable willed to his son in 1751. The last name of Boston was common among blacks and those with that last name included the famous black Nantucket whaling captain Absolom Boston. Yarmouth historian Daniel Wing noted that Mary's mother, Lucy, was a full-blooded Native American.

Mary Dunn was of mixed race, half black and half Native American. There was a close relationship between blacks and Native Americans in the years up to the Civil War, and they were often grouped together in the public mind. There were few pure-blooded Native Americans left in the Yarmouth area during Mary's time. Daniel Wing wrote, "In 1797, there was left standing one wigwam only [in South Yarmouth]; it was on the banks of the river, and was occupied by a squaw and a Negro." The Negro in Lucy's wigwam was not Boston Boston, as he had died soon after Mary's birth.

Town records show that Lucy married another black man, Cato Judah on April 16, 1786. Cato Judah may have been the slave Mrs. Lucy Bourne of Yarmouth put in her will of 1782. The will "gave her Negro boy Cato to her son Richard" and stated that "when Cato arrived at 35 years, her son shall manumit him." According to town records, Lucy and Cato had two more children, Richard born in 1786 and Betsey born in 1789.

Mary's Adult Life

On January 4, 1807, Mary Boston married Thomas Dunn, with Reverend Timothy Alden of Yarmouth officiating. Thomas Dunn and family are listed in the 1810 Barnstable census under the column, "All other free persons," a column used only for nonwhite inhabitants. The records of the East Parish Church stated that Dunn worked as a fisherman out of Barnstable Harbor and was lost at sea in the summer of 1832. As such, her husband could not have been a former slave, partial to the South, who recruited local Cape boys for the Confederacy.

Thomas and Mary Dunn took care of black and Native American indigents in their home, which was on the shore of what is now called Mary Dunn Pond in Hyannis. Mary sold spirituous liquors out of her home. She was known to brew "yarb beer," a colloquial term for herb beer. It may in fact have been fermented herb tea. There are many stories of Mary's famous potent concoctions.

The 1810 census lists two in Thomas Dunn's household. Mary and Thomas had at least one child, a daughter named Lucy. The *Yarmouth Register* reported on July 25, 1839: "Died—In Barnstable, Miss Lucy Dunn, daughter of the late Thomas Dunn." This was collaborated by Thomas Stetson's journal entry dated July 23, 1839, which read, "going with the hearse to Mary Dunn's daughter funeral $1.00. All other charges 75 cents."

The Dunns did not own property in Yarmouth or Barnstable. Nothing in the Registry of Deeds lists their names. Most likely, they were squatters on land belonging to Zenas Basset, probably what is now the northeast corner of the Hyannis Airport. An 1887 deed on the land makes the first known reference to Mary Dunn's Road.

By 1846, Mary was a pauper, as she was given supplies that year by Barnstable's overseers of the poor. The overseers preferred to let the poor dwell at home and help them, rather than remove them to the town's almshouse. This enlightened view ultimately led to Mary's death. Her house burned in 1850 and she died in the blaze.

Swift unwittingly combined the lives of Mary Dunn and Lizzie Blatchford, also known as Lisa Tower Hill, who lived in the area and died in 1790. Where Swift got the story that Mary Dunn was "found prostrated with stupor, with a large adder entwined around her neck and one on each ankle in the wild wood" is anyone's guess.

Obtaining information about "common folk" who lived two hundred years ago is never easy. In Mary's case, several documents enable us to track her life. It doesn't need embellishment. Mary was a caring person who helped others who were less fortunate. A road with her name on it is a constant reminder that people of all types contributed to the rich history of Cape Cod. Mary Dunn Road, located

The Cultural Center on Old Main Street, South Yarmouth. This is the location of the last Native American teepees in South Yarmouth. Mary Dunn was born in this area.

Mary Dunn Pond. Mary lived near a pond, now named in her memory. The pond is just off of Mary Dunn Road in Barnstable.

halfway between the villages of Barnstable and Yarmouth Port connecting Route 6A with Hyannis, and Mary Dunn Pond are a tribute to the folklore of Mary Dunn.

LIZZIE BLATCHFORD (LIZA TOWER HILL)

Lizzie Blatchford was born about a hundred years before Mary Dunn. Born Elizabeth Lewis, she married William Blatchford when she was just sixteen years old. The Blatchford's family came from the Tower Hill section of London and Lizzie became known as Liza Tower Hill. They settled near Half-Way Pond, which later became Mary Dunn Pond.

Liza led a solitary life. Because of her strangeness—the fact that she helped to cure animals and save crops—there is much folklore surrounding her.

The woods near the pond where Liza lived were known as the "Enchanted Forest" by nearby residents. Rumors had it that Liza danced on the pond's surface and animals in the area were strangely deformed. A cloven-footed rabbit, luminous fish and swamp devil goats were just some of the animals supposedly seen. People traveling the road, especially at night, swore that Liza put bridles and saddles on them and rode them all over the Cape. The forest had luminous stumps and this only helped the stories grow. Perhaps it was the effect of the liquor one could buy from Liza that caused the forest to seem "enchanted."

Sailors thought Liza turned into a cat that swam after their vessels. It was stated that when her cat was shot, Liza Tower Hill died. Her daughter, Lydia, worked as a servant for the Allyn family. For years after her death there were rumors of Liza's house being haunted

Mary Dunn moved into this area while the stories and memories were still vivid. These most likely contributed to the folklore of Mary Dunn.

CAPE COD INDIANS

Most historians believe there were fifteen Native American villages making up the native community on Cape Cod. In addition, they believe each village was its own tribe. This is not the case. The fifteen villages were part of a larger nation that included all of Cape Cod and lands north to Boston and south to the Narragansett Bay. The Native Americans of this area were know as the "Pokanok" or "people of the bays." The native village of Mattakeese was made up of the town of Yarmouth and surrounding areas. During the 1800s, most of the remaining Pokanok (then known as the Wampanoag) lived within three reservations: the Massapee Reservation, the Bass River Reservation and the Herring Pond Reservation. The Bass River Reservation became know as Indian Town. Due to their beliefs and religion, there is much folklore on the mystical powers of the Native Americans.

28 STRAWBERRY LANE

The Indian Spirit

There are three ponds not far from 28 Strawberry Lane. These ponds may well play a role in the happenings of 28 Strawberry Lane. The larger pond, Greenough Pond, is on land where the Native American Thomas Greenough moved when he left Indian Town in South Yarmouth. At least one person who has experienced unexplained happenings or spirits feels the pond and nearby hill may have been a burial or ceremonial site. It is not hard to conceive the notion that Native Americans may well have lived on the land of 28 Strawberry Lane.

The spirits, cloaked figures that appear when a person is in bed, are hard to distinguish. Other times, birdcages appear to be hanging from the ceiling. Sometimes dried flowers have been seen floating above the bed.

The effect on the person witnessing this phenomenon is one of an unsettled feeling, sometimes bordering on fear. Sometime the feeling one gets is of unhappiness. Those who have witnessed this think the spirit itself is unhappy, which might well be the case for a grieving ghost of someone departed. The dried flowers could be an offering to the memory of the departed.

Native Americans believed the spirit of the individual would rise above the body and enter an afterworld filled with birds, animals and flowers. The vision of birdcages and dried flowers suggest a burial ground may be nearby.

More than one person has witnessed the strange and unexplained events of 28 Strawberry Lane. These include doors that opened and closed by themselves, and lights being turned on and off without anyone touching the lights or switches. Some might maintain that these things happen in old houses; others are far more suspicious of each unexplained action.

ELISHA NAUHAUGHT

Deacon Elisha Nauhaught, a Christian Native American, lived in South Yarmouth. He was so honest that even the devil couldn't tempt him. Folklore has it that the devil offered Elisha a "lost" bag of gold coins if he would provide favors for him. Nauhaught, financially poor, took the coins and returned them to the rightful owner.

This angered the devil, who sought revenge. He ordered a den of black snakes to attack Nauhaught. They attacked, wrapped around his legs and prevented any escape. The lead snake slithered up the native's torso, reached his face and peered into Nauhaught's mouth. Nauhaught, not afraid, bit off the snake's head. The other snakes reacted out of fear and quickly left. The devil never bothered Nauhaught again.

The poet John Greenleaf Whittier wrote a poem about the deacon, who is buried near the Native American memorial along Long Pond in South Yarmouth.

The Indian Memorials in South Yarmouth. This is the final resting area of the last full-blooded Native Americans in Yarmouth. There are no gravestones and the marker was placed here much later.

A NATIVE AMERICAN VISITOR

Several years ago, a builder purchased a tract of land in Harwich to build a home for himself. Before undertaking his project, he researched the history of the land. It was rumored to have had some Native American connection. After thorough investigation, he found neither a burial ground nor any other historical significance to the property.

After the house was built, he and his family moved in. When fall came, he began working outdoors, clearing the dead brush from the area near the marsh. The landscaping was planted over time.

On most nights, the owner usually fell into bed exhausted. It was on one of those fall nights that he was awakened from a deep sleep by something. There was a vision in his bedroom doorway. She was just watching him. He could tell she was an older Native American woman by her clothing. She just stood there for a while and then disappeared.

The native woman appeared many times during that fall. The builder had a sense that she had been observing him repairing the land and had approved. No one else in his family experienced her visits. She may have been buried nearby and felt herself to be the caretaker of this land.

It has been said that Native Americans believe that their ancestors coexist with people today, but on a different plane. Earlier generations of the tribe inhabit this very space, but on an alternate tier, with a fine veil separating the past from the present. Perhaps this woman slips through time to check on her property.

BITS AND PIECES

WHAT ARE GHOSTS?

There are two theories put forth by those who have written about ghosts. The first states that ghosts are merely the energy left behind after a person dies. These ghosts normally don't interact with their "viewers." Their "images" never change and appear as just a fleeting glance.

The second theory states that the soul lingers as a spirit in a place the person was either familiar with or in which he died. These ghosts are active and are usually credited with mysterious activities, such as the playing of music, the rearrangement of articles, changes in temperature and apparition sightings. They may also leave behind physical evidence of their visits.

Some people who claim to have seen ghosts believe that you should speak to them. By speaking to them, you may help them resolve whatever issues caused them to be present.

Do not be surprised if you are given a "cold shoulder" and your visitor simply disappears.

To see ghosts, look in the area of your peripheral vision. Ghosts are most frequently seen there, and they disappear when looked at directly. Older lore suggests that you see ghosts better over your left shoulder, or when looking in a mirror with another person.

You don't believe in ghosts? It is said that if a doubter takes a child under the age of ten with her, they are far more likely to have a successful experience. The child will see the ghost!

SUPERSTITIONS

Ghosts and superstitions go together. Many of the old superstitions are tied to the prevention of ghostly tricks. Cape Codders, up through the nineteenth century, were a very superstitious lot. Some of their beliefs included:

1) Never slam a door—you might hurt a ghost.
2) Bells drive away ghosts because they don't like loud noises.
3) If a candle's flame suddenly turns blue, a ghost is nearby.
4) A bride's veil protects her from spirits who are jealous of happy people.
5) Clinking glasses of alcohol together before you drink knocks the demons from the glass.

6) Brooms have special ways to attract ghosts. Don't lean a broom against a bed—it will invite spirits to the bed.

7) Never bring a broom with you when you move—throw it out or leave it behind and buy a new one.

8) Looking in a mirror by candlelight is one way to see a ghost.

9) To protect your house from ghosts coming in, plant juniper, rosemary or ivy near the front door. Ghosts (and witches) feel they have to count every leaf, get frustrated that there are so many and leave.

10) Young girls should cut their hair only during the young of the moon. Fewer ghosts are present during new moons and freshly cut hair is one place spirits try to enter your body.

11) A cricket in the house brings good luck.

12) Your mother always told you to cover your mouth when you yawn. She knew that doing so kept spirits from entering your body when your mouth was open. (And you thought it was just being polite!)

PREVENTIVE MEASURES

An Old Shoe

Our ancestors used many things to ward off ghosts and spirits from their homes. Aside from superstitions, few remedies remain. On occasion, one may surface—in this instance, a shoe. When the owners, Paul and Susan Cook, of 323 Union

A horseshoe for luck above a door on Winter Street, Yarmouth.

Street, South Yarmouth, were renovating, they discovered a shoe stuck in the wall near the chimney. The shoe appears to be from the time the house was built—perhaps an early Quaker shoe.

There is an old English superstition, brought to the colonies by the settlers, which stated that a shoe placed in the rafters or near the ovens in the chimney would ward off evil spirits—some call it the "evil eye." The hiding of a shoe while a house was under construction was called concealment. Today, most people are unaware of early folklore and thus, when renovating old homes, they aren't looking for items of spiritual interest. The Society for the Preservation of New England Antiquities (now Historic New England) ran an exhibit of old shoes. One concealment shoe from a New England home was included in the exhibit.

This isn't the only concealment shoe that has been found in Yarmouth. At least two others have been identified. One was a worn moccasinlike shoe from the same era as the one found at 323 Union Street. A second was found during a major renovation of a sea captain's home built in the 1840s. This shoe had a hard leather sole and looked to be the type worn during the period in which the house was constructed.

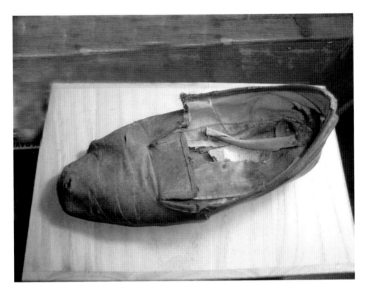

The concealment shoe found at 323 Union Street, South Yarmouth. This worn shoe was discovered during renovations. *Photo courtesy of Paul Cook.*

A SPIRITED SALE

There is a house near the two banks on Old King's Highway that has had reports of ghosts. The most recent report came from the summer of 2005, when children who were visiting told their mother of seeing and hearing ghosts. The former owners told friends they had sold the house because of the spirits.

OUR THANKS

Staying the Night

A young couple was driving through a rural part of Yarmouth in a Model T Ford late one night, looking for a place to stay. They were on sandy roads and they kept getting stuck. The husband, tired of continually digging to free the wheels, told his wife they would stop at the next lighted house.

A small Cape Cod house soon appeared with a light on in one window. The husband got out of the Model T and knocked on the door. An elderly man opened the door, just slightly, and the driver explained their predicament—they were lost, tired and needed a place to stay.

The elderly man's wife came to the door and invited them in. "We haven't much, but you're welcome to use the spare room which has a bed," she said. Then she busied herself finding something to feed them for dinner.

The young people were obviously embarrassed by the attention, but they needed a place to stay and offered to pay. The elderly couple wouldn't hear of it. "That's not neighborly," the woman told them. "Someday you can repay the favor to someone else."

The young couple said they were leaving early the next morning and asked the owners not to get up with them. After all was agreed, they retired for the night.

Early the next morning, the travelers arose and quietly prepared to leave. The young wife insisted they leave money in an envelope as a way of saying thanks. An envelope, with the words "Our Thanks" and a five-dollar bill inside, was left on the table near the front door.

The couple proceeded about a mile down the road and found a general store that sold gasoline and food. They related their tale to the store owner, who looked at them incredulously.

"You couldn't have stayed at the house you say you were at," he stated with a finality that surprised them both.

"Why not?" asked the young wife.

"Well, that house burned down six months ago, and both of the old people died in the blaze. People got stuck in the sand trying to get to the fire, and by the time they arrived, both were dead."

After buying some provisions, they turned the Model T around and headed back to the house where they had stayed. They were shocked to find the house had indeed burned, although no one had torn it down. Wandering inside the front door, they noticed an envelope on the badly charred table. In large letters was written, "Our Thanks."

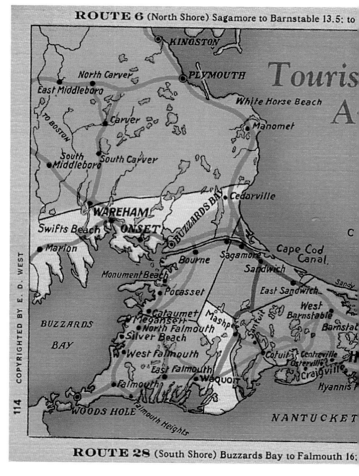

A 1930s postcard of roads on Cape Cod. Tourists prior to World War II often used postcards as maps as there were far fewer roads. The driver of the Ford probably relied on just such a map.

Bits and Pieces

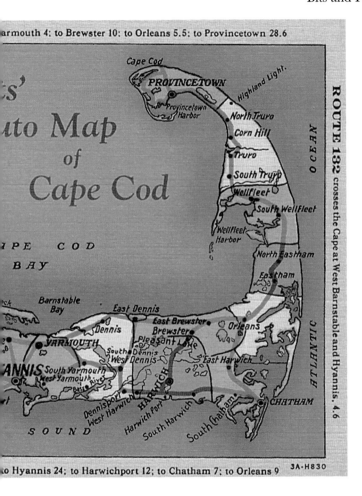

217

SOURCES

We have prepared this list of the sources that we used so that you will know where to look if you are interested in more information. The list does not include articles on death and dying, which came from many different places; citations for Edward Gorey's books (he wrote over a hundred); or the articles that have appeared in the *Yarmouth Register*, written by members of the Historical Society of Old Yarmouth.

BOOKS

Albright, Evan. *Cape Cod Confidential: True Tales of Murder, Crime and Scandal from the Pilgrims to the Present.* Yarmouth Port, MA: On Cape Publications, 2004. Cape Cod stories of murder and intrigue.

Barber, Laurence. *When South Yarmouth Was Quaker Village.* Yarmouth Port, MA: Historical Society of Yarmouth, 1988. This book chronicles the story of the South Yarmouth Crooked House and Dr. John Stetson.

Botkin, B.A. *A Treasury of New England Folklore.* New York: Crown, 1947. A number of great stories—much more off-Cape myths and legends.

Braginton-Smith, John, and Duncan Oliver. *Port on the Bay: Yarmouth's Maritime History on the "North Sea" 1638 to the Present.* Yarmouth Port, MA: Historical Society of Old Yarmouth, 2001. This contains the story of moving the Native American and African American graves at Ancient Cemetery on Center Street.

Bray, Ella. *All Around the Common.* Yarmouth Port, MA: Historical Society of Old Yarmouth, 1978. She states that every house but one that sits on the Yarmouth Port Common is haunted.

Canning, John, ed. *50 Great Ghost Stories.* New York: Bell Publishing Co., 1971. Contains ghost stories from around the world.

Crosby, Katharine. *Blue-Water Men and other Cape Codders.* New York: Macmillan Co., 1946. This contains the only known references to Aunt Sophie Ann Kelley Chase.

Gordon, Dan, and Gary Josephs. *Cape Encounters: Contemporary Cape Cod Ghost Stories.* Hyannis, MA: Cockle Cove Press, 2004. This contains the story of #361 Route 6A.

Jasper, Mark. *Haunted Cape Cod and the Islands.* Yarmouth Port, MA: On Cape Publications, 2002. This contains stories of Colonial House Inn (on Route 6A next to the Edward Gorey house), the Old Yarmouth Inn (p112) and 418 Route 6A.

———. *Haunted Inns of New England.* Yarmouth Port, MA: On Cape Publications, 2000. This contains stories of two Yarmouth Inns: Liberty Hill Inn (77 Route 6A) and Old Yarmouth Inn (223 Route 6A).

Reynard, Elizabeth. *The Narrow Land: Folk Chronicles of Old Cape Cod.* Boston: Houghton Mifflin, 1968. Her book is the best compilation of myths and legends on Cape Cod. If you ever see it, buy it. This mentions Midsummer's Eve, the time of ghost ships.

Swift, Charles. *History of Old Yarmouth.* Yarmouth Port, MA: self-published, 1884. The standard history for looking up things about Yarmouth.

WEBSITES

Cape and Island Paranormal Research Society, www.caiprs.
 com.
Colonial House Inn, www.colonialhousecapecod.com.
Old Yarmouth Inn, www.oldyarmouthinn.com.

Visit us at
www.historypress.net